With the right methods men can accomplish something noticeable, but not necessarily eternal. With the right empowerment they can truly change the world and bring about eternal fruit—and the method matters little. In this book, Steve Smith lifts the hood and shows us the real secret behind apostolic, disciple-multiplying movements... and it isn't a strategy, workbook, program, or 5-step plan. It is something all of us have instant access to and which promises to bear eternal fruit. It is time we welcome the Holy Spirit and follow His lead into the harvest fields.

Neil Cole
Apostolic missionary and author of many books including *Organic Church*, *Church 3.0*, *Journeys to Significance*, and *Primal Fire*

Steve Smith has dedicated his life to the fulfilment of the Great Commission through movements that multiply disciples and churches. He has made a significant contribution to our thinking on strategy and effective methods. But Steve knows best practice is not enough. Now in *Spirit Walk* he explains how God's power is available to work in us and through us for his glory and the discipling of the nations.

Steve Addison
Author, *Pioneering Movements: Leadership that Multiplies Disciples and Churches*

The vast majority of Christians in America live with a sense of low-grade frustration. The main reason behind this sense of frustration is simple: Christians tend to depend upon their own power and not the power of the Spirit. That is a recipe for failure. Steve Smith's book *Spirit Walk* is a practical, powerful guide to combat this satanic scheme. This book could well change your life!

Jeff Wells
Senior Pastor of WoodsEdge Community Church (Houston Metro Area)

I knew *Spirit Walk* was special when I kept on stopping to reflect on the biblical candor and battle-tested wisdom from the first couple of thousand words. Steve Smith is one of the key pioneers in Kingdom movements. In this book, he puts a spiritual laser on the divine fingerprints observed on every one of the hundreds of 21st century movements, and he invites Christ followers not to try to lead the parade but pursue and abide in God.

Jerry Trousdale
Director of International Ministries, New Generations
Author of *Miraculous Movements*, co-author of *The Kingdom Unleashed*

Sooner or later most pastors and missionaries come to the end of their rope and realize the best preaching, methodology, training, and strategy does not result in something that can only be explained by the power of God. Steve Smith shares from his personal pilgrimage and seeing the Spirit of God work on the mission field how every Christian can experience a "Spirit Walk" as the norm in daily victorious living and ministry.

Jerry Rankin
President Emeritus, International Mission Board, SBC

Steve Smith reminds us that walking in the Spirit is indispensable to every significant Kingdom breakthrough over the past 2,000 years. I commend all readers to this powerful resource for their Kingdom journey.

David Garrison
Executive Director, Global Gates

This is a groundbreaking book for all of us who care about the mission of God in the earth…. Steve Smith is one of the men that has truly shaped the Antioch Movement as well as thousands of others' lives. His leadership, strategic mind, and absolute commitment to the love and power of

God make him a man worthy to follow. I am so proud of Steve and his new book *Spirit Walk*. I believe it will be another move forward for all of us who truly are desiring His Kingdom to come and His will to be done in our lifetime.

Jimmy Seibert
Senior Pastor of Antioch Community Church and President of Antioch Ministries International

In the last few years, I have had the opportunity to know Steve Smith personally, and have come to admire the strength of his faith, the humility of his leadership, and the simplicity of his ministry methods. Reading his work in *Spirit Walk* has shown me why he is such a high-impact leader in our generation. His primary method of doing ministry is to walk and work in the power of the Holy Spirit. That is exactly where Steve is inviting us to go: not to depend on our smart strategies but to go back to the Book of Acts, experience a life of grace and power, and produce much fruit. He is offering this book to show us how. I promise your life and ministry will not be the same if you apply the principles outlined in the book.

Dr. Bekele Shanko
President, GACX and VP of Global Church Movements, CRU

Steve Smith is a missionary, church planter, and eager disciple of our Lord. As you will discover, his heart beats with the urgent necessity of living each day in the fullness of the Holy Spirit.

Tom Elliff
Former President of the International Mission Board (IMB) and Founder of Living in the Word Publications

Some Christians live as if the Holy Spirit does not exist. Others have been taught non-biblical extremes. This book will help you biblically understand the Holy Spirit AND give you practical ways to daily be filled with the Spirit and then live each hour in the power and guidance of the Holy Spirit. I would highly recommend this book for all of us who want more of God.

Stan Parks
Co-facilitator 24:14 (2414now.net), VP of Beyond (beyond.org), trainer and coach for various CPMs

Steve provides a clear introduction to an issue which is central to living an abundant and fruitful life for our King and His Kingdom.

Curtis Sergeant, disciple

Before Jesus Christ's crucifixion, resurrection, and ascension, He promised that we would do "greater things" than He did while He was on the earth (John 14:12). In *Spirit Walk*, Steve Smith reminds the church that these "greater things" can only be accomplished by the power of the Holy Spirit at work within the people of God. I found his tangible instructions on how to embark on mission with the Spirit moment-by-moment incredibly inspiring to my personal ministry as well as to my leadership of a team of Spirit-indwelt and Spirit-empowered missionary leaders.

Kurt Nelson
CEO, East-West Ministries

Today we have to be able to complete the Great Commission of the Lord Jesus. The most important thing is for every believer to become a [person] of power filled with the Holy Spirit. Only in this way can the gospel of the kingdom be preached throughout the world as a testimony to all nations. Thank God! This book can lead us to walk with the Holy Spirit daily.

Ying Kai
Executive Director, T4T Global Missions

Steve Smith has done it again with another essential book for completing world evangelization. His *T4T* book gave us the methodology for fostering movements. Now in *Spirit*

Walk, he gives us the essential companion book by which we may cultivate the power of the Spirit in our lives and ministries. Great methods will only take us so far, but combined with the work of the Spirit, there is no limit to what God can do. It is a must-read for every serious follower of Jesus.

Rick Wood
Editor, Mission Frontiers Magazine

Spirit Walk is a refreshing, biblical view of what it means to "walk in the Spirit." In a world full of chaos and tension, we are quick to operate in our own strength. However, the biblical principles in *Spirit Walk* provide a guideline to lead by looking to the Holy Spirit to guide us.

Mario Zandstra
President, East-West Ministries

There is a deep hunger in most of us to see God show up with explosive Kingdom power as He uses us. We hear about it happening—mostly in other places, with other people. *Spirit Walk* takes us beyond the "shoulds" and "oughts" of being filled with the Spirit to showing how it is compellingly simple to attain. Using Jesus as our model, it is intensely practical, and yet costly. This was a convicting read, like a knuckle grinding into my ribs—ouch!

Carol Davis, mission strategist and mobilizer

God has already used Steve Smith in mighty ways for His Kingdom. And now *Spirit Walk* comes at a time when the church desperately needs Christ-followers who are deeply connected with the Spirit. Prayer has always been a bedrock of our church's ministry, and yet God is giving us a fresh vision for the power of prayer in evangelism. Steve's book is a big exclamation point on what God has been revealing to us. I highly recommend it for all believers who are hungry to see breakthrough in their lives—breakthrough from sin and spiritual apathy, as well as Kingdom breakthrough to a lost and troubled world. The principles found in this book hold the key to unlocking the power of the Gospel as we take up our God-given mandate to be His ambassadors to the ends of the earth.

Bryant Wright
Senior Pastor, Johnson Ferry Baptist Church, Marietta, GA
Former president of the Southern Baptist Convention

As believers, every aspect of our lives every day is dependent upon walking in the power of the Spirit. We cannot be effective spouses, parents, disciplers, or church planters without this reliance on the Spirit. This book is a must-read for every believer in order to realize the full potential of the life God has in store for us.

Jeff Sundell, Chief Field Strategy Officer
e3 Partners

In *Spirit Walk*, Steve Smith maps out a practical path for engaging with God in every step of life. His acronym ("S.W.A.P."), the backbone of the book, really works for me. I guess the greatest measure of a book is the growth we gain by reading it. I grew personally from *Spirit Walk* and I can't wait to apply its teachings.

Doug Lucas
President of Team Expansion, and Founder/Editor of Brigada

Do you long to move beyond the ordinary to the extraordinary? *Spirit Walk* is practical biblical teaching on walking in the fullness of the Spirit every hour of every day. Rather than shortcuts, Steve teaches us the ancient paths that lead us out of defeat to the great works God wants to accomplish in and through us.

John Becker
Director of Ministry, AIM; International Coordinator, Vision 5:9

Spirit Walk

Spirit Walk

**The Extraordinary Power of Acts
for Ordinary People**

Steve Smith

*If we live by the Spirit, let us also
keep in step with the Spirit.*
Gal. 5:25

2414 Ventures is a boutique publisher focused on printing books about finishing the Great Commission through kingdom movements. While 2414 Ventures blesses and supports the global network called "24:14 Coalition," it is not organizationally connected to that movement. The names of both are coincidental—related to the commitment of both to the fulfillment of Matthew 24:14.

To dear brothers and sisters laboring in faith for Acts-like church-planting movements across the world. Together, may we fulfill Matthew 24:14 and 28:18–20 in the power of the Spirit.

TABLE OF CONTENTS

SET SAIL WITH THE SPIRIT

A Wind is blowing across the face of the Earth.

More tumultuous than the mightiest hurricane. More powerful than the vortex of a swirling tornado. No living thing can stand before its assault. Kingdoms fall. Excuses fail. Hearts open.

The gale sweeps forward.

No locked door of opportunity stays shut.

No obstacle of worldview slows it.

Its eddies swirl into the corridors of any closed mind.

This Wind is more life-giving than the sweetest breath. From Adam until now, its exhalation gives life to any person. Its gust dresses dry, bleached bones in spiritually living flesh. Its mighty rush rests flames of power upon followers of Jesus.

This zephyr has launched the ships of every movement of God in history. Disciples of Jesus are sent out, riding the waves of its force beyond the rims of every horizon.

Distant peoples kneel before its melodic sound as waves lap on the shores of their nations and currents of air swirl through their valleys.

Believers are stirred from slumber into mighty awakenings by this Wind. First a faint draft. Then a steady breeze. And finally a swirling typhoon of life. Revival comes again—spiritual re-living.

Continuing its eons-long journey, this breath now sweeps across another generation of panting followers of Jesus.

No man tames this tempest.

No human controls this zephyr.

No meteorologist forecasts its direction.

No nation is exempt from its blowing; no community devoid of its wafting.

No movement arises apart from its power.

No method bears fruit apart from its life-giving breath.

No willpower transforms apart from its infilling.

Yet multitudes of believers, church leaders and theologians forget its power. Generational amnesia spreads among us. We forget how the Wind has blown in the past. Instead, we reason that the Wind no longer blows today, or we relegate reports of this "power" to brands of the Christian church that make us feel uncomfortable.

But the gale has never stopped or slackened. It is rushing and swirling around you if you will open your eyes.

This Wind has a name:
πνεῦμα
Pneuma
Spirit
Holy Spirit, to be exact.
The undervalued and misunderstood
third Person of the Trinity.

The words in the New Testament for "spirit" and "wind" are the same. All of life began by the Spirit, the Wind of God, hovering over creation.

> In the beginning, God created the heavens and the earth. The earth was without form and void, and darkness was over the face of the deep. And *the Spirit of God was hovering over the face of the waters.* (Gen. 1:1–2, emphasis added)

Today, overwhelming stress and anxiety run rampant. We are inundated with information, burdened by the pace of life, and often find ourselves tangled in the web of over-stimulation. But we must remember that the Wind of God's Spirit blows as strongly today as it did hovering over the waters of creation. Its force never wanes, for this is the Spirit of God Almighty.

Take comfort in the fact that this Wind is not an "it" but a "Him." He is a Person who wants a relationship with you. One in which He controls you, for you cannot control Him any more than you can control the wind. He is Almighty God.

The Wind of the Spirit is blowing powerfully in all the nations of the six populated continents. Within those nations, two types of Jesus-followers dwell: those who fail to see or hear the Wind—and therefore fail to move with Him—and those who allow the Wind to engulf them, learning how to move with the Spirit. Those who allow the Wind to blow through them often experience a complete transformation of their lives and the lives of people around them.

When the Spirit shows up in power and the people of God surrender to His sweet leadership, awe-inspiring movements of God emerge. Every revival in history has ridden the waves of this unstoppable combination: Hearts surrender to an all-loving, almighty Spirit. Character transforms. Doors open. Fruit emerges. Unimaginable dreams become reality.

The Wind is blowing. You are a spiritual sailor with two options:

1) You can raise the sails of your ship and position them so you can move with the Spirit toward the destinations God has designed.
2) You can leave the sails down, keep paddling in your own strength, and surrender to the tides drawing you backwards.

No matter your choice, you cannot make the ship of your life move in the right direction without Him. You cannot force the ship of enduring ministry fruitfulness to stir. You can only raise the sails. God must blow. But the good news is He *is* blowing. He waits for you to raise the sails so you may move with Him.

Doubtless you are familiar with Jesus's words that you must be born again to become a new creation—a son or daughter of God. But have you keyed into His words five verses later?

> *The wind [Spirit] blows where it wishes, and you*
> *hear its sound, but you do not know where it comes*
> *from or where it goes. **So it is with everyone who is***
> ***born of the Spirit.*** (John 3:8, emphasis added)

Moving with Him is mysterious. It means following His unpredictable but delightful ways. It is a journey you will never regret. It is a quest that fulfills the longings of your heart.

In hundreds of places across the six continents disciples are returning to their original design. The DNA of Jesus's discipleship is emerging fresh. Disciples are making disciples. Churches are starting churches. Leaders are maturing into their God-appointed roles.

> " IN HUNDREDS OF PLACES ACROSS THE SIX CONTINENTS DISCIPLES ARE RETURNING TO THEIR ORIGINAL DESIGN. **THE DNA OF JESUS'S DISCIPLESHIP IS EMERGING FRESH.** "

The Book of Acts is happening again and again and again.

At the core is not a method (though simple, biblical methods are important). At the center is not a discipleship process (though life-on-life interaction is critical).

What is driving and sustaining the explosive growth of God's kingdom is the age-old Spirit Walk God designed us for. Disciples are learning to keep in step with the Spirit of the Almighty God who knows no boundaries, opens every closed door, and produces fruit that lasts for eternity.

The key to the fruitful life you were designed to walk in is in living in right relationship with the Spirit of your Creator. Methods meet obstacles. Processes encounter breakdowns. Only the Spirit can move you through the standstills in life and ministry. He is the Spirit of breakthrough.

Take the journey to plumb the depths of Scriptures to explore the mystery of walking with the Spirit. Allow yourself to be led by the Wind. Let the Word of God remove the fears that plague the edges of your awareness. Let the loving Father assure you that His presence brings peace, not anxiety.

Learn to take the Spirit Walk daily.

It is an unpredictable path with predictable steps.

From the beginning of history, the Spirit Walk was the path you were created to take. Abiding in Him was God's plan from the beginning, not an add-on or afterthought for the Christian life. Genesis began with the Spirit bringing life to the waters of creation and breathing life into Adam.

In the middle of history, Jesus stood, arms stretched out wide, calling in a loud voice:

> *"If anyone thirsts, let him come to me and drink. Whoever believes in me, as the Scripture has said, 'Out of his heart will flow rivers of living water.'" Now this he said about the Spirit, whom those who believed in him were to receive, for as yet the Spirit had not been given, because Jesus was not yet glorified.* (John 7:37–39)

At the end of history, the Spirit remains the theme—the only way the final generation will complete God's mission. The last chapter of the Bible ends with the call to drink from the life-imbued waters of the Spirit:

> *The Spirit and the Bride say, "Come." And let the one who hears say, "Come." And let the one who is thirsty come; let the one who desires take the water of life without price.* (Rev. 22:17)

From beginning to end, the Bible paints a theme: the Almighty creates us for His purpose, and we, His creation, fulfill that purpose relying upon His life-giving Spirit.

Every spiritual awakening in history has started this way: the Spirit Walk.

Will you take the predictable steps for the unpredictable path?

The Wind is blowing. Do you dare raise your sails and join in the journey?

INTRODUCTION

My wife and I had been working in Asia for fifteen years, and in that time we saw the Spirit of God work in power in ways we had not experienced when planting a church in North America. We were experiencing a movement of multiplying disciples and churches and were seeing the Word spread quickly. It felt like the Book of Acts was replaying itself in front of our eyes. We were eventually coaching movements on virtually every continent of the world.

A pastor who visited one of our trainings in Asia asked if we could bring this training to America. My wife and I were immediately on board. Over the course of four days, four hundred pastors, church planters, and mission leaders gathered to examine the Word of God and ask one overarching question: how can we cooperate with the Spirit of God to see Him work powerfully in America again—not just in Asia or Africa?

This particular training with four hundred church leaders proved to be a watershed moment in North America.

The Spirit of God met with us afresh. In this time, many leaders renewed their commitment to emulate what the Bible describes as the norm for discipleship. Six years later, many of us point to that meeting as a turning point in disciple-making movements emerging in cities across North America.

What really struck me was that, from the beginning, we could tell God was doing something big, and that the global North was ready to listen. In fact, on the first day of this meeting, during the break, my wife overheard a woman talking to a friend. She said, "I was telling someone that I was coming to a church-planting conference. She asked me, 'Which one? Willow Creek? Saddleback? Another one?' But I told her 'None of these. The meeting I'm attending is about how church planting has virally spread from places like China.'" The woman continued, "My friend exclaimed, 'China?! God is really working in China. We should pay attention to that.'"

My wife could hardly wait to share this news with me. After all, it pointed to an incredible truth—after centuries of darkness, *Asia was teaching America*. The gospel that had progressed from the Western world to Asia was now educating the Western world about its power to change. The powerful movements of the Spirit in Asia were reminding the Western world about its own roots. Roots that were well understood a few generations ago. Roots formed by the Holy Spirit moving among us in our original awakenings and in subsequent revivals.

The Hidden Mover

At the end of the 1990s, I could count on two hands the number of Acts-like movements around the world. At the time of this publication, we are tracking more than six hundred of these movements—on every continent, in churched *and* post-churched societies.

It's not that Asia has discovered something new. Rather, it has rediscovered something *ancient*—forgotten ways of discipleship that were the norm in other generations and places.

Not only in Asia and Africa but in the cities of the Western world, God is now moving in fresh and unprecedented ways. We are seeing record numbers of baptisms among never-churched, broken people. Churches are being revitalized. Lives are being transformed. Relationships are being healed. Communities are finding hope.

The Book of Acts is exciting. To see Acts *again* today is thrilling as we watch God at work—the God that is the same yesterday, today, and always (Heb. 13:8).

But we must be careful. In our sincere desire to see God move in our personal lives, our churches, and our ministries, our first recourse is often to examine the *methods* behind what is going on. The methods are important. I have written other books about the biblical principles and methods that God is using to multiply disciples, churches, and leaders all over the world.[1]

---

1 See, for example, Steve Smith with Ying Kai, *T4T: A Discipleship Re-Revolution* (Monument, CO: WIGTake Resources, 2011).

But that should not be where we look *first*.

Rather, the Hidden Mover behind every movement is the Holy Spirit. He is the *assumed* but often *not discussed* force in our work.

No More Assumptions

In my several decades of experience, I have come to understand one vital truth. Assuming that disciples and workers in the kingdom understand how to walk daily in the power and guidance of the Holy Spirit is dangerous ground. Holy Spirit illiteracy

HOLY SPIRIT ILLITERACY **ABOUNDS AMONG LONG-TIME CHRISTIANS.**

abounds among long-time Christians.

I therefore no longer assume anything.

Too often we assume that Christians understand what it means to be filled with the Spirit or to walk by the Spirit. Pastors throw out the phrase "be filled with the Spirit" but there is a lack of clarity among followers of Jesus about what that actually means.

You, an ordinary person, were designed to walk in the extraordinary power of God we see in the Bible. But do you know how to do that?

If we live by the Spirit, let us also keep in step with the Spirit. (Gal. 5:25)

Stop for a moment and ask yourself one question: "Do I clearly understand what the Bible teaches about how to be filled with the Spirit repeatedly, and am I walking it out daily?" *If there is any lack of clarity or resolve, this book is for you.*

We must no longer assume that Christians understand the basics of walking in the Spirit. Spiritual amnesia has gripped large numbers of Christ-followers and the epidemic is spreading. Large swaths of believers have forgotten the ancient ways of the Spirit Walk.

This book is about the biblical principles of walking in the power of the Mover behind movements like those now happening on every continent. The late Dr. Bill Bright with Campus Crusade used to teach students *first* to learn to be filled with the Spirit, *then* to learn the discipline of personal evangelism. Personal evangelism was the method behind people coming to Christ, but the filling of the Spirit was the power behind the method.

This is not something new or revolutionary. In fact, Jesus set His disciples on this path originally, commanding them to wait until they were filled with power from on high, then to be His witnesses (see Luke 24:48–49; Acts 1:8).

This book is about the power behind the methods. A power we assume will be there when we need it but one that many of us are strangely ignorant about.

This book is about the spiritual force behind transformation to Christlikeness and ministry fruitfulness, a force we assume should empower us, but is largely lacking.

But let me put this in perspective. I was not raised in a charismatic or Pentecostal environment. This book on (repeatedly) being filled with and walking in the Spirit is not coming from a Pentecostal. I have been a Southern Baptist evangelical from the days of nursery.

Baptists are not particularly known for their understanding and emphasis on being filled with and walking in the Spirit daily. In fact, most Baptists I know are a bit afraid of the Holy Spirit. We want Him but we keep Him at arm's length. But all believers in Jesus—no matter their theological flavor—must learn to rely on the Spirit. We ordinary followers must learn to live by the extraordinary power of Acts.

For forty years, I have been in the school of Jesus, learning how to walk in the Spirit. Since the practice of the Spirit was not a natural part of my discipleship, I was forced back to the pages of Scripture, sometimes over the objections of well-meaning leaders. I wanted to understand how disciples must *biblically* be filled with the Holy Spirit over and over again. Not wanting to follow strange winds of doctrine, I pored over the pages of my Bible to comprehend how the Spirit should guide us each day. With bands of intrepid fellow disciples, I learned to pray and humble myself before God so that He could show me how to live every moment.

I am not perfect. Too often I revert back to *my own* control rather than *God's* control. You are catching me at my current stage on a journey that will be finished when I see Jesus face to face. But I *am* on the journey and invite you to join me on the same journey—the ancient journey of the Spirit Walk.

That is what this book is all about—giving up control of our lives to the right Influencer. Not to harmful influences, substances, or willpower but rather to the Eternal Influencer.

Making the Spirit Walk Standard Operating Procedure

This book does not assume our modern generation understands how to walk by the power of the Spirit daily. When personal lives are in disarray, morals decline, relationships and marriages break apart, churches split, and ministries lack fruit, the signs point to our generation growing in spiritual amnesia and declining in the Spirit Walk.

But Acts-like movements around the world remind us that the Spirit Walk is alive and well in many places. The pages of Scripture and examples of these Acts-like movements are calling you to rediscover the forgotten ways of walking in the Spirit. The Spirit Walk must not be relegated to one theological viewpoint but must be standard operating procedure for every child of God.

The pages of this book will pull back the curtain to allow you to see and experience what disciples in the New Testament understood all too well. This book takes you behind the scenes to understand how the Spirit of God is moving in great power around the world and how He can move in your life and ministry.

Walking in the Spirit should be the most *natural* aspect of our *supernatural* life. Unfortunately, it is actually the *missing* element of many Christians' lives. I find that there is no end to those who are unclear on what the Bible teaches about this. When you are unclear on the Spirit Walk, then other things (including yourself) are in control of your life. This is a powerless discipleship walk and fruitlessness is the result. The result is ordinary people living by *ordinary* power, not the *extraordinary* person of the Spirit.

To make up for the lack of the Spirit's control, we resort to props for growing in our Christian walk and ministry: devotional books, online media, worship videos, well-ordered programs, church attendance, theological studies, good works, self-help approaches, and ministry workshops. These are not bad things and can *all* be used by the Spirit in our discipleship. But none of them is a *substitute* for your daily reliance upon the Holy Spirit.

Clarity about the Path Forward: S.W.A.P.

In these pages, we will simply and systematically lay out a clear roadmap for learning the ancient path of the Spirit Walk: to daily be filled with the Spirit and then live each hour in the power and guidance of the Holy Spirit. Using this approach, you will undoubtedly rediscover what has been forgotten in our age.

The roadmap will be lifted from the pages of Scripture. We will lay out a simple framework to understand the biblical principles and commands of walking in the Spirit. We will organize these principles into four broad categories using a simple acronym that can help you call them to mind each day: how you can S.W.A.P. your control for God's control continually. Here are the basic principles:

Surrender to His will and His every word
Wait on God in prayer
Avoid sin, and let God root out all unrighteousness
Pursue the promptings of the Spirit

S: unconditional **surrender** to God's will and His every word. The first step in learning to walk in the Spirit is to surrender completely to Him. The wineskin of your life must be emptied of the water of self before it can be filled with the wine of the Spirit.

W: **waiting** on God in prayer. Time after time, disciples in the Scriptures were filled with the Spirit after a period of waiting on God in prayer. For God to act afresh upon you, you must wait on Him, and this happens most often in prayer.

A: **avoiding** sin in your life. If the Holy Spirit is truly holy, then He must dwell in a holy vessel. As you wait upon God in prayer, He wants to root out any sin in your life to make your heart a comfortable and welcoming home for Him.

P: **pursuing** the promptings that the Spirit will give when He fills you. Disciples in Scripture *always* proved that the Spirit filled them by how they responded. The Holy Spirit will continually prompt you in the relationship about where to go, what to think, what to do, and what to say. He will always prompt you to live for God's purposes. Learning to walk in the Spirit is about learning to follow His promptings each hour. Then you are abiding in Christ.

S.W.A.P. is not necessarily *sequential*. These are not four steps in a process that you can follow in order, nor do you *have* to. Rather, they describe four biblical activities or postures that God will use to help you become filled with the Spirit and then walk in the Spirit. I personally find that "S," "W," and "A" happen simultaneously and eventually lead to "P."

Chapter by chapter, this book will explain each of these four elements and give you guidance on how to implement them in your life. Disciples in earlier days understood these four basic principles and implemented them regularly. We, however, have a different set of circumstances, living in a world that sometimes seems powered by sin. Between social media, technology, and a social climate that seems increasingly hostile to living in faith, our work is cut out for us. But these principles must become second nature to a new generation, regardless of the challenges we face.

Posturing Your Life to Receive from God

Each of these four biblical principles is a spiritual discipline or exercise to help you surrender your heart to the control of God each moment of each day. Disciplines help you posture your heart to receive God's grace.

S.W.A.P. is a spiritual posture for the Spirit Walk.

A posture helps you accomplish certain objectives in your daily life. For example, a posture of lying down and counting sheep helps you experience the power of sleep.

In the same way, spiritual disciplines help us posture our hearts to interact with God.

S.W.A.P. is a simple framework to understand the postures that specifically help you be filled with the Spirit afresh on a regular basis and then follow His guidance. You need the power of God in your life daily—for personal Christlikeness, for relationships, and for the good works to which God has called you. God has saved you and left you in this world to make a difference.

The voice of the Spirit need not seem distant.

The power of the Spirit need not feel blocked.

S.W.A.P. will give you a succinct, clear understanding of what the Bible says about the Spirit Walk. Just like exercising a muscle makes it stronger, so learning to S.W.A.P. daily will enable you to learn to walk in sync with the Holy Spirit. In the beginning, you will revert frequently to your own control. But as you exercise your S.W.A.P. muscles, you will develop longer and longer periods of staying under God's control, not yours.

Together, as we S.W.A.P. our control for His, with multiplying disciples from movements around the world, we are calling you to join us in the ancient Spirit Walk. No matter their background—Christian, Muslim, Hindu, atheist, Buddhist, animist, postmodern—broken people are joyfully becoming whole again and courageously rescuing other broken people. It's all happening through the Great Overcomer who sets us free from bondage and empowers us for God's purposes in this world. Join us in this movement by adopting these daily postures and your life will be forever changed.

A Call to All

This book is not for members of mainstream, evangelical, charismatic, or Catholic churches. It is not for Christians of western Christendom, Asia, or the global South. It is not for missionaries, pastors, or new believers. Let's drop the labels.

It is for disciples of Jesus. Period.

We must *all* learn this ancient discipline that is called the Spirit Walk.

The ancients understood it. They call you to join in the ancient paths.

The multiplying disciples in movements today call you to the Spirit Walk as well.

The ancients teaching Asia. Asia teaching the Western World.

Grab your intrepid band and come join us.

Questions to Ponder

Stop now and write down the names of several friends that you believe would want to take this journey with you. Friends who will open their hearts to whatever the Bible says. Friends who will be honest with you and each other. Friends who want Jesus more than life itself—or *want* to want Jesus more than life itself.

_____   _____

_____   _____

_____   _____

_____   _____

Contact them today and invite them to this journey. Help them get a copy of this book and together learn how to take the steps into the amazing spiritual landscape where the heavenly Guide will lead you. Read two or three chapters a week and then get together to discuss them, pray together, and make applications for your lives.

CHAPTER 1

PREDICTABLE STEPS FOR AN UNPREDICTABLE PATH

Jesus taught his disciples to pray this simple command to their heavenly Father: Cause Your kingdom to come on earth as in heaven! (Matt. 6:10).

For two thousand years since then, Jesus-followers have learned that prayer, the Lord's Prayer, by heart. Our Father's heart is that His reign will come fully to our homes, our neighborhoods, our nations. He wants to reign supreme in power in every place through hearts surrendered to Him.

Every day, a myriad of disciples around the world pray that God's kingdom will come fully. But when we pray for this, do we really mean it?

On every continent, transformation is sweeping communities, declaring victory over demonically controlled lives. Acts-like movements are bursting forth in people groups and cities as ordinary believers return to the fundamental DNA of biblical discipleship. As Christ-followers begin to live as disciples were always meant to live, they experience the power of the Spirit in their personal lives and ministries. Once this happens, discipleship becomes a fact of life. But until God's kingdom breaks loose in a community, gospel efforts will never keep pace with population growth. The transforming power of the Book of Acts must emerge again and again to keep up.

Countless followers of Jesus long to live victoriously over sin and circumstances—to grow in Christlikeness. Yet for many, this way of life remains elusive. Strongholds remain. Christian maturity seems a long way off. Personal transformation sputters, though that's not the only challenge. Transformation of communities, cities, and people groups remain beyond the grasp for many.

Yet the number of Acts-like kindgom movements proliferates across the globe. How to walk in step with God to catalyze "kingdom come" (at home and abroad) is the question of the hour. How do we truly multiply disciples and churches?

Three areas emerge as essential in the process of personal and communal transformation: (1) biblical **paths** or methods that any believer can follow, (2) discipleship **processes** to equip believers to walk those paths, and (3) a spiritual **posture** of reliance upon the Spirit of God to empower the process. Whether it is overcoming a stronghold in our personal lives or in catalyzing the multiplication of disciples, these three areas are essential. However, the secret to every

> " ...THE SECRET TO EVERY FRUITFUL LIFESTYLE AND MINISTRY IS NOT PRIMARILY IN METHODS OR PROCESSES **BUT IN THE SPIRIT OF GOD**. "

fruitful lifestyle and ministry is not primarily in methods or processes but in the Spirit of God.

Not by might, nor by power, but by my Spirit,
says the LORD of hosts. (Zech. 4:6)

The Spirit Walk.

Many earnest believers want the path (an effective ministry or lifestyle tool) and the process (a weekly life-on-life discipleship model) and assume that the spiritual depth and vitality in themselves and their groups are in place. They know they need better accountability and more purposeful structure and often *assume* that these will solve issues: bondages to wrong lifestyles, lack of evangelism results, shallow discipleship, a paucity of meaningful relationships, and sputtering multiplication of groups. In other words, they view a method, a program, and a pattern as the core.

These elements *are* important for real transformation.

But assume nothing.

Never assume that the spiritual posture is in place to breathe life into these approaches. Paths and processes *should* work but not if they are devoid of the power of God. Only the Spirit Walk enables good strategies—whether in personal life transformation or in plans to change the world.

Holding to a form of godliness, although they have
denied its power. (2 Tim. 3:5, NASB)

From the beginning, Jesus defined His own ministry in this way:

> *"The Spirit of the Lord is upon me,*
> *because he has anointed me*
> *to proclaim good news to the poor.*
> *He has sent me to proclaim liberty to the captives*
> *and recovering of sight to the blind,*
> *to set at liberty those who are oppressed,*
> *to proclaim the year of the Lord's favor."*
> (Luke 4:18–19, emphasis added)

Jesus wanted it to be clear that the Spirit of God and the favor of God characterized His personal life and mission. He described Himself as clothed with, covered by, or overflowing with the Spirit. Jesus was a person dressed with the Spirit. Just as He modeled baptism, He also modeled to His disciples what a Spirit-led daily walk looked like.

Unlike the legalistic religious leaders of His day, Jesus did not simply hold to a *form* of godliness. He had its power. He embodied the Spirit Walk, from beginning to end.

Two thousand years later, the ancient path remains the same. We must turn back from any legalistic or human-empowered version of religion and ministry that emphasizes forms and patterns apart from the power of God.

The Turning Point in Acts

After three years of *personally* shaping them by His physical presence, Jesus gave His followers a clear command for how they would continue His mission. In addition to charging them to make disciples by baptizing them and teaching them to obey all He commanded them (Matt. 28:18–20), He exhorted them *not* to start that process until they had received power from on high.

> *"You are witnesses of these things. And behold, I am sending the promise of my Father upon you.* **But stay in the city until you are clothed with power from on high.** *"* (Luke 24:48–49, emphasis added)

> *"But* **you will receive power** *when the Holy Spirit has come upon you, and you will be my witnesses in Jerusalem and in all Judea and Samaria, and to the end of the earth."* (Acts 1:8, emphasis added)

He set them on the ancient path of the Spirit Walk. In their three years with Jesus on earth, the apostles frequently missed essential points or squandered ministry opportunities. But their spiritual perspectives changed in Acts 2 on the Day of Pentecost. The filling of the Spirit (and the repeated filling of the Spirit) was the turning point in the lives and ministries of the disciples.

Over the last twenty years, I have led believers around the world through an in-depth study of Paul's journeys to learn from his example and apply these principles in our ministries. Invariably, the primary observation that emerges is that, while Paul had a clear path of ministry and strong discipleship processes, he was led by the Spirit. Paul knew what to do but the Spirit showed him where to do it, with whom, and in whose strength.

> *And they went through the region of Phrygia and Galatia, having been **forbidden by the Holy Spirit** to speak the word in Asia. And when they had come up to Mysia, they attempted to go into Bithynia, but **the Spirit of Jesus did not allow them**. So, passing by Mysia, they went down to Troas. And a vision appeared to Paul in the night: a man of Macedonia was standing there, urging him and saying, "Come over to Macedonia and help us." And when Paul had seen the vision, immediately we sought to go on into Macedonia, concluding that God had called us to preach the gospel to them.* (Acts 16:6–10, emphasis added)

> *Him we proclaim, warning everyone and teaching everyone with all wisdom, that we may present everyone mature in Christ. For this I toil, **struggling with all his energy that he powerfully works within me**.* (Col. 1:28–29, emphasis added)

Paul and his team lived the very way Jesus predicted they would: the Spirit Walk. An unpredictable path paved with predictable steps.

The wind blows where it wishes, and you hear its sound, but you do not know where it comes from or where it goes. So it is with everyone who is born of the Spirit." (John 3:8)

Remember, the word "wind" and "spirit" are the same word in the Greek. Just as we cannot predict the direction of the wind, so we cannot predict the direction God will take us as we implement the principles of His Word.

Breakthroughs and movements emerge when we follow the pathways God has prepared, not those we try to create ourselves. No matter how many disciples we make or groups we start, at some point we stall if He is not in full control. If the Spirit does not guide us to the people He has prepared, we are spinning our wheels. You can have a perfect model for evangelism and follow-up discipleship, but if you don't find the God-prepared people, fruit remains small. You may win individuals to Christ, but you fail to find the breakthrough people who will lead many to salvation—people like the Samaritan woman, Cornelius, and the Philippian jailer.

His Spirit is blowing in your life, opening doors to bring real life transformation—if you will let Him. Your job is to surrender to His purposes and empowerment. We must trust that the key to every miraculous transformation is not us. If you are paralyzed by feelings of personal inadequacy or hobbled by pride, there's a simple solution. Turn the attention from yourself back to God. His work has never depended upon you but only upon Him. He loves to use you when you surrender to His Spirit within you.

> *What then is Apollos? What is Paul? Servants through whom you believed, as the Lord assigned to each. I planted, Apollos watered, but God gave the growth. So neither he who plants nor he who waters is anything, but only God who gives the growth.* (1 Cor. 3:5–7)

His Spirit is also moving all around you to open the hearts of people. Your job is not to prepare their hearts. Your job is to find the people God has opened and then to disciple them, revealing paths they can walk in *and* lead other new disciples down. Just as you have the Teacher living in your heart, tutoring you in Christlikeness, so do they. It is your duty to trust the Spirit of God in them and help them respond to Him.

The Turning Point in Every Historical Awakening

Just as the filling, guiding, and empowerment of the Spirit were the focal points of the book of Acts, so also has it been in every revival and awakening in history. Churches everywhere cry out that our world needs fresh awakening. We beg for awakening, and yet we neglect the central elements that are required for this miracle to emerge.

One overarching characteristic of these movements in history has been an outpouring of the Spirit of God upon the people of God based upon the Word of God. How do we return to such a phenomenon? Although movements are obviously a work of God, there are essential ways that the people of God can cooperate with God to help facilitate this.

The sails of a sailboat do not propel it forward; the wind does. Yet a wise sailor knows to raise the sails so that as the wind blows, the boat can move forward. And as the wind blows, the sailor knows to adjust the sails to keep the boat moving with every shift of the wind.

Awakenings in history have often occurred as God's people humble themselves in a way that responds to His Spirit. They raise the sails of their lives and call upon the Wind of the Spirit to blow.

During one of the awakenings in England and America (starting in the 1830s) thousands of revival prayer groups were overwhelmed by the power of the Spirit. In 1858 during the American portion of this revival, ships drawing near American ports came within a "zone of heavenly influence."

Ship after ship arrived with the same tale of sudden conviction and conversion. In one ship a captain and the entire crew of thirty men found Christ out at sea and entered the harbor rejoicing. Revival broke out on the battleship *North Carolina* through four Christian men who had been meeting in the bowels of the ship for prayer. One evening they were filled with the Spirit and burst into song. Ungodly shipmates who came down to mock were gripped by the power of God.[2]

---

2 Arthur Wallis, *In the Day of Thy Power: The Spiritual Principles of Revival* (London: Christian Literature Crusade, 1956), 77.

The **Welsh revival** in 1904–1905 swept 100,000 people into the kingdom. It was marked by unusual outpourings of the Spirit of God upon ordinary believers as they surrendered to God.

In the famous **Shantung (Shandong) Revival** (1927–1937) in China, Southern Baptist missionaries, in no way Pentecostal in theology, moved into an era of extreme conviction of sin, experiencing true awakening as they confessed themselves and surrendered to God's purposes. The Spirit of God was poured out on them afresh. This movement swept throughout the missionary community and the Chinese Church paving the way for the modern Christian movement in China.

Around the world today movements continue to sweep through nations and people groups. In each movement, the Spirit of God empowers believers to live out the essence of discipleship, to make disciples who can do the same, and to form Acts 2 churches, which are white-hot in their worship of God. Apart from the fullness of the Spirit, no movement emerges. We must take the Spirit Walk—daily. It has always been Plan A.

Banishing Fear

We have all heard of strange things that occur when people say they have been filled with the Spirit: barking like dogs, laughing like hyenas, rolling around on the floor, and so on. But a true, biblical Spirit Walk is the very opposite. A careful examination of Scripture will help you achieve the walk without the worry. Since the Holy Spirit is the Spirit of Jesus (Acts 16:7), you will not become weird. You will become like Jesus. Knowing Scripture with your heart banishes all fear, replacing it with the knowledge and understanding of your walk in Him.

A brother in ministry described to me his upbringing in a Bible-believing church. Functionally, his church's view of the Trinity was Father, Son, and Holy *Scripture*. He was never taught about the Holy Spirit, much less how to be full of the Spirit.

As a child, I believed in the Holy Ghost, but I was terrified of anything called a ghost. As I grew older and hungrier for the Word of God, I held the impression that "being filled with the Spirit" was something only Pentecostals do. How tragic that many Bible-believing Christians around the world let fears of what they have heard keep them from walking in

> WE LET PENTECOSTAL EXTREMES AND CHARISMATIC EXCESSES ROB US OF **THE JOY AND POWER OF WALKING IN THE SPIRIT**.

the Spirit. We let Pentecostal extremes and charismatic excesses rob us of the joy and power of walking in the Spirit.

Many Pentecostal brothers and sisters fall into another ditch, sometimes relying upon one-time or occasional powerful experiences rather than an ongoing walk in the Spirit.

Other Christ-followers fail to take the Spirit Walk for fear that they will become "mystics" who do not live by the eternal truths of the Bible but by mysterious impressions and promptings. They worry that they must assume strange postures and weird disciplines that open them up to demonic influences such as in Eastern mysticism.

Fears and misperceptions blind us to the biblical clarity of the Spirit Walk.

And so, millions of Christians live defeated lives—defeated in overcoming sin, defeated in relationships, defeated in church life, defeated in personal ministry.

Only the Spirit Walk can change the equations that enable the kingdom to come on earth as in heaven.

The Spirit Walk is simply letting the Holy Spirit become *the* guiding force in your life, ministry, church, and organization day by day. **This book attempts to describe and prescribe a biblical path for walking in the fullness of the Spirit every hour of every day. Period.**

If we truly are people of the Bible then we should be *biblically* filled with the Spirit. Hearsay and experiences do not provide the guide for the Spirit Walk. Only the Bible does.

The Key to a Movement in You and through You

A great and godly missionary leader has noticed a change in missionaries over the last fifty years. As a senior citizen, in recent years he has spent much of his time at a training center that prepares missionaries for service. He said, "When I was a young missionary, fifty years ago, I met many *spiritual giants*. But when it came to kingdom movements, we were *methodological pygmies*."

But after fifty years of change, he made this observation: "Today I meet a lot of young missionaries who are *methodological giants*, yet they are *spiritual pygmies*."

If we must have one or the other, let us be spiritual giants. But can we not be *both* methodological and spiritual giants? A tendency grows among disciple-makers, church planters, pastors, and missionaries to focus on methodology in their ministries. And in our personal walks with Jesus, bookstores abound with "5 Simple Steps to…" books. Simple, reproducible methodologies that new believers can live out *is* critical to personal godliness and a movement of God around us—but methods are mere mechanics without the Spirit of God.

> **BUT METHODS ARE MERE MECHANICS WITHOUT THE SPIRIT OF GOD.**

There is no shortcut to great works of God in us and through us. Apart from the fullness of the Spirit there is no lasting fruitfulness. Sandwiched within three chapters on abiding in Christ and being full of the Spirit is this verse:

> *You did not choose me, but I chose you and appointed*
> *you so that you might go and bear fruit—fruit that*
> *will last—and so that whatever you ask in my name*
> *the Father will give you.* (John 15:16, NIV)

Of the twenty-one chapters in the Gospel of John, three of them deal with the indwelling Holy Spirit (John 14–16). Fifteen percent of the Gospel of John is on the subject of living your life in the Spirit! The bulk of Jesus's last conversation with His disciples in the upper room prior to His crucifixion was about the coming of the Holy Spirit and His impact on their lives.

Jesus could have focused on the methods and processes He had modeled for His disciples. He could have made lists and gone over action items. Instead, He described for them the utter importance of relying on the coming Spirit and the fruit that would emerge from this relationship.

> *"Truly, truly, I say to you, whoever believes in me will also do the works that I do; and **greater works** than these will he do, because I am going to the Father.... And I will ask the Father, and he will give you another **Helper**, to be with you forever, even the Spirit of truth, whom the world cannot receive, because it neither sees him nor knows him. You know him, **for he dwells with you and will be in you**."* (John 14:12, 16–17, emphasis added)

The Father wants to do great works in and through each one of us. Yet this will not happen apart from the Helper who is the Holy Spirit. Until we cultivate a life in which He dwells within us and fills us in every way, we will not see fruitfulness in our personal lives or in our ministries.

On my desk is a beautiful calligraphy print that my wife gave me to remind me where strength comes from and to whom glory should go:

Not by might, nor by power, but by my Spirit,
says the LORD of hosts. (Zech. 4:6)

Several years ago, the Lord made it clear to me never to assume that the spiritual vitality of Jesus-followers is in place. He forbade me to train disciples to multiply disciples and churches without emphasizing the majesty of God and the power of the Spirit in a surrendered life. Today, I make no assumptions.

The Spirit Dwells in You, but Does He Dwell in Fullness?

Miss Bertha Smith was a missionary in China during the Shandong Revival. In the latter years of her life she roamed the halls of Southwestern Baptist Theological Seminary in Fort Worth, Texas. She tried to pass on the spirit of the revival to students around her. She would often corner a student and ask one simple question. "Are you full of the Spirit today?"

Frankly, such a question evokes a feeling of awkwardness almost as strong as Miss Bertha standing in front of you, her finger in your chest. It may be a question that makes you cringe, but truth is often rooted in your discomfort. Putting yourself in that place of discomfort is the only way to truly hold yourself accountable each day.

This is the question we all must confront. The question is not "Have you ever been filled with the Spirit?" The question is "Are you full of the Spirit today?"

Yesterday's filling is no guarantee for today. The

> THIS IS THE QUESTION WE ALL MUST CONFRONT. THE QUESTION IS NOT "HAVE YOU EVER BEEN FILLED WITH THE SPIRIT?" **THE QUESTION IS "ARE YOU FULL OF THE SPIRIT TODAY?"**

effects of past experiences do not necessarily linger. How things were yesterday does not guarantee how they'll be today.

The Spirit Walk requires you to surrender each day.

One foundation undergirds a correct theology of the Spirit Walk: when you come to Christ, you are sealed with the Spirit of God.

> *In him you also, when you heard the word of truth,*
> *the gospel of your salvation, and believed in him, were*
> *sealed with the promised Holy Spirit.* (Eph. 1:13)

A seal implies permanence and promise. God has made you His son or daughter if you have trusted Christ as your Lord and Savior. You *are* a new creation. The old is gone. The new has come (2 Cor. 5:17). His Spirit has taken up residence in your life. You are forever sealed with the Spirit, and He promises never to leave you. But remember, being sealed does not mean being filled. And being filled in the past does not mean being full today. The filling of the Spirit is a repeated, continuous faith walk that we must cultivate our whole lives.

Jesus comes to us through His Spirit so that we are never alone, never orphaned:

I will never leave you nor forsake you. (Heb. 13:5)

I will not leave you as orphans; I will come to you. (John 14:18)

One of the most common biblical descriptions of the Christian is that we are "in Christ":

There is therefore now no condemnation for
those who are in Christ Jesus. (Rom. 8:1)

Part of the richness of this description is that your life is now united with Christ and your spiritual life is hidden in Him, protected by Him, and empowered by Him. You belong to Christ. You are no longer your own. Every believer clearly has the Spirit of God within him or her. You do not receive Him later.

You, however, are not in the flesh but in the Spirit, if in
fact the Spirit of God dwells in you. Anyone who does not
have the Spirit of Christ does not belong to him. ¹But if
Christ is in you, although the body is dead because of sin,
the Spirit is life because of righteousness. (Rom. 8:9–10)

At salvation, you received the Spirit of God who will never leave you. But that is not the same thing as being full of the Spirit and letting Him control you in power moment by moment.

Before the day of Pentecost, the disciples of Jesus did not have the indwelling Holy Spirit. They were unable to walk in the guidance and power of the indwelling Spirit hour by hour. Prior to Pentecost they seemed to miss ministry opportunities at times or even revert back to old ways.

But after the day of Pentecost, all of the equations changed because of the filling of the Holy Spirit. They continued to use the same methods Jesus taught them, but now they began to bear greater fruit. Peter and John very likely went to the temple each day at the hour of prayer. But in Acts 3, after receiving the power of the Spirit, they noticed a lame man sitting by the gate—a man they had probably passed unnoticed many times. After the filling of the Spirit, the radar of the Spirit was strong in their lives. They noticed him and in faith healed him. The result was that many people believed which fueled a budding movement in Jerusalem.

The fullness of the Spirit always bears fruit in the lives of surrendered disciples. Even full-time Christian workers need to repeatedly return to the basics of the Spirit Walk.

Although the Spirit Walk does not guarantee a movement of God such as in Acts, a movement of God will not come in you and through you *apart from it*. Since the Spirit is God (and we are not), He will take us in directions we never imagined. But these directions will all be consistent with His Word, the Bible.

> *The wind blows where it wishes, and you hear its sound, but you do not know where it comes from or where it goes. So it is with everyone who is born of the Spirit.*" (John 3:8)

The Bible gives clear guidance on how to submit to the Spirit so that He guides us daily wherever He leads.

This book will guide you into a life of surrender. It outlines predictable, biblical steps for an unpredictable path! There is no shortcut apart from the fullness of the Spirit.

Questions to Ponder

1. What fears or misperceptions have kept you from fully embracing the Spirit's leading? How has reading this chapter changed your understanding?
2. If you have trusted Christ as your Savior, the Spirit indwells you. Do you know if He has ever filled you (for a first time or a fifty-first time)?
3. Since yesterday's filling is no guarantee of today's, are you full of the Spirit today? Would you like to be?
4. What steps can you take today to get started in your Spirit Walk? (Suggestion: pray now for courage to take this path.)

CHAPTER 2

SPIRIT WALK

The walk in the Spirit is unpredictable, though the Bible supplies predictable ways for us to surrender ourselves to His leading. But what does this walk really look like? While we know the term "walk in the Spirit," what does that actually mean?

It all starts with understanding who the Holy Spirit is.

Filled with What or Whom?

What are we being filled with when we say we want to be filled with the Spirit?

The Holy Spirit is not a cosmic force as in Star Wars.

The Holy Spirit is not a power to be channeled.

The Holy Spirit is not a low-level spirit that becomes your spiritual guide.

The Holy Spirit is *God Almighty*. He is one of the three persons of the Godhead along with the Father and the Son.

The Holy Spirit is a person, not an impersonal force. The Holy Spirit is a "he," not an "it."

That detail is key. Understanding that the Holy Spirit is a *person* is a vital part of learning how to walk in fullness of the Spirit. You must remember that this is a *relationship* and you must treat this relationship as you would relationships with other persons.

Perhaps it will be easier if we remember that the Holy Spirit is, in essence, *the Spirit of Jesus.* In John 14, Jesus promises to return to His disciples after His ascension in the form of the Holy Spirit.

Twice in the New Testament the Holy Spirit is called the "Spirit of Jesus":

> *And when they had come up to Mysia, they attempted to go into Bithynia, but the **Spirit of Jesus** did not allow them.* (Acts 16:7, emphasis added)

> *For I know that through your prayers and the help of the **Spirit of Jesus Christ** this will turn out for my deliverance.* (Phil. 1:19, emphasis added)

While some believers have reservations about the Holy Spirit, they like the person of Jesus. Most of us would love to have Jesus physically hang out with us. Can you imagine what it would have been like to sit in the same room with Jesus? To eat a meal with Jesus? To ask Him any question you wanted? We envy the original disciples who shared life with Jesus in that way for three years.

Yet the Holy Spirit represents *the person of Jesus* coming in spirit form to each one of us. He brings the presence of Jesus to us just as tangibly as if we could see Jesus standing before our eyes. He is the *Spirit of Jesus* in each of our lives. You do not need to fear the Holy Spirit because He is just like Jesus. Banish from your mind any fears. As you walk in the Spirit, you will demonstrate the spiritual character and fruit of Jesus. What the Spirit wants to do is to fill you, guide you, and mature you into a complete Christlike person.

Though you are in Christ, *Christ wants to be fully in you*:

> *To them God chose to make known how great among the Gentiles are the riches of the glory of this mystery, which is Christ in you, the hope of glory. Him we proclaim, warning everyone and teaching everyone with all wisdom, that we may present everyone mature in Christ. For this I toil, struggling with all his energy that he powerfully works within me.* (Col. 1:27–29)

The Holy Spirit is the presence of Jesus coming to live in you and walk with you. The third person of the Trinity represents the Father and the Son to us. He comes alongside us and walks with us just as Jesus walked with His disciples in physical form. Rather than run from the Spirit, run to Him just as you would to the arms of Jesus.

What Does Being Filled Really Mean?

You can have the Holy Spirit *in* you and still not be *full* of him. He can dwell in you but not necessarily fill you. Dwelling and filling are two different aspects of the same relationship. Christ is in you, but does He have *all* of you?

In every language, terms and phrases carry connotations— sometimes positive and sometimes negative. For instance, the term "Spirit-filled Christian" brings certain ideas to your mind. Often that phrase is used to describe someone who claims to have had a "second blessing" of the Holy Spirit in traditional Pentecostal theology. It can become a label or a denominational tag.

The term "being filled with the Spirit" has become so common that it has become cliché. We assume people know what we mean by it and often they (or you) are too embarrassed to ask for an explanation. Other scriptural terms that describe the same aspect of Christian living can shed light on the meaning of this phrase.

The Bible gives three parallel terms to describe the same experience:

> **Abiding in Christ =**
> **Being filled with the Spirit =**
> **Letting the word of Christ**
> **richly dwell within you**

Understanding these other phrases will help you understand the fullness of the phrase "be filled with the Spirit."

Abiding in Christ

In the upper room, as Jesus ate the Last Supper with His disciples, He taught them about the coming of the Holy Spirit who would become their Helper. In John 14 and 16 Jesus spoke clearly about the Holy Spirit. Sandwiched between these two chapters, in John 15, He shifted the narrative from the Helper to Himself. He described Himself as the true vine and every disciple as a branch that must abide or live its life in Him.

> ***Abide in me***, *and I in you. As the branch cannot bear fruit by itself, unless it abides in the vine, neither can you, unless you abide in me. I am the vine; you are the branches. Whoever abides in me and I in him, he it is that bears much fruit, for apart from me you can do nothing.... **If you abide in me, and my words abide in you**, ask whatever you wish, and it will be done for you. By this my Father is glorified, that you bear much fruit and so prove to be my disciples.* (John 15:4–5, 7–8, emphasis added)

The word "abide" means to "remain in," "dwell in," "live in." In the Greek, it means to "remain in a place" and figuratively to "remain in a sphere." Jesus makes it clear that the disciples must live their lives completely in Him and in the life-giving power that comes from Him. Apart from that posture, they can bear no fruit.

Jesus is the sphere in which we must live our lives. The only lasting things we become and produce are from doing what He is doing. Apart from his life-giving sap flowing through us by His spirit, nothing will greatly change in us and nothing great will emerge in our ministries.

Jesus makes it clear in John 15:7 that we will know if we are abiding in Him if His Word is completely dwelling in us. When His Word fills our minds and controls us, then we live by *His* leadership. Living in Christ and His Word living in us is the essence of letting the Holy Spirit fill and guide us. Why? Because the Holy Spirit *is* the Spirit of Jesus.

> " LIVING IN CHRIST AND HIS WORD LIVING IN US IS THE ESSENCE OF LETTING THE HOLY SPIRIT FILL AND GUIDE US. WHY? **BECAUSE THE HOLY SPIRIT IS THE SPIRIT OF JESUS.** "

Abiding in Him as the Vine of John 15 becomes reality through abiding in Him as the Helper (Holy Spirit) of John 14 and 16. Jesus is the vine. Our lives must be grafted in Him and only the sap of His words can give us life. Any attempt at spiritual existence apart from Him, or only half-way connected to Him, is fruitless and frustrating. His sap flowing through us is the Spirit filling us with the Word of God.

Being Filled with the Spirit

Being filled with the Spirit is another way to describe abiding in Christ. The most familiar passage about being filled with the Spirit is found in Ephesians 5:

> *And do not get drunk with wine, for that is debauchery,*
> *but **be filled with the Spirit**, addressing one another in*
> *psalms and hymns and spiritual songs, singing and mak-*
> *ing melody to the Lord with your heart, giving thanks al-*
> *ways and for everything to God the Father in the name*
> *of our Lord Jesus Christ, submitting to one another out of*
> *reverence for Christ.* (Eph. 5:18–21, emphasis added)

While Jesus used the picture of a vine and branches, Paul uses another metaphor here to describe the same spiritual reality: that of a vessel or wineskin. Paul explains that our minds are under the influence of something. Is it spirits (wine) or the Spirit?

Something is always controlling and filling us. The question is *what* is filling us. A person's mind can be controlled by his own selfish will, another person, an ideology, a demonic power, or the Spirit of God. It may be hard to believe, but we have the power to choose which fills us, but it doesn't just happen. We must work for it.

Suppose that you want to fill a water bottle with pure red wine. To do that you would have to empty the bottle of what fills it currently—the water. Once it is empty, only then could you fill it to the top with wine.

In the same way, Paul is describing that we must be filled with the right substance. We must not be under the influence of the wrong things. Alcohol, for instance, which clouds our judgment, should not be abused. Instead, we must be completely filled with and under the influence of the undiluted Spirit of God. Paul describes the same reality as the one Jesus was describing. We are absolutely controlled by God and His Word through the person of the Spirit when we allow Him to fill us.

Letting the Word of Christ Richly Dwell within You

The third picture, which parallels the other two, is the word of Christ living in us fully. The metaphor now switches to that of a house. In this house, the words of Christ fill every room.

The metaphor of a house in Colossians 3 is a parallel metaphor to that of the wineskin in Ephesians 5. Both start with a different command yet end with similar results.

	Colossians 3:16–18 HOUSE	Ephesians 5:18–22 WINESKIN
Command	¹⁶ **Let the word of Christ dwell in you richly**,	¹⁸ And do not get drunk with wine, for that is debauchery, but **be filled with the Spirit**,

Results

teaching and admon-ishing one another in all wisdom, singing psalms and hymns and spiritual songs, with thankfulness in your hearts to God. [17] And whatever you do, in word or deed, do everything in the name of the Lord Jesus, giving thanks to God the Father through him.
[18] Wives, submit to your husbands, as is fitting in the Lord.

[19] addressing one another in psalms and hymns and spiritual songs, singing and making melody to the Lord with your heart, [20] giving thanks always and for everything to God the Father in the name of our Lord Jesus Christ, [21] submit-ting to one another out of reverence for Christ.
[22] Wives, submit to your own husbands, as to the Lord.

The results of each action are virtually identical: speaking to one another in psalms, hymns, and spiritual songs; giving thanks to God in all things; submitting to one another. If you read only the bottom portion (results), you would think that these were almost identical passages. But the commands, the starting points, are different on the surface. In Ephesians, the command is to be filled with the Spirit. In Colossians, the command is to let the word of Christ dwell in you richly.

These two commands describe the same reality. They simply use different word pictures: a *wineskin* being filled with the right substance and a *house* being filled with the right occupants. Being filled with the Spirit is no different than letting Christ's words live in us. We open every room of our lives to Him and His Word. No corner is off limits.

If there are rooms locked away from the control of God's Word, then Jesus is not dwelling in us fully. He is a limited occupant. We still retain the keys and the control of our lives. We are the landlord.

For example, you may surrender to Jesus to be the Lord of your devotional times. You set your alarm to awaken thirty minutes earlier than usual to spend time in the Bible and in prayer before heading to work or to school. You have started unlocking part of your life to His control.

But if you allow God to speak only to that area of your life, He is still a limited occupant. If you choose to be involved in relationships that are not healthy and God-honoring, the Spirit does not have that room of your house. If you allow your thoughts to run rampant, He does not occupy that room. If you hoard your possessions or use belittling words, He is not occupying those rooms either.

So, in your quiet time, you have started the day with good intentions—to hear from God and seek Him earnestly—but you have left the Spirit in that corner of your life. You started by abiding in Christ but quickly stopped abiding the rest of the day.

When that is the case, you are not being filled with the Spirit. His Word is not controlling each sphere of your life.

Our minds and hearts must be completely saturated with the words of Jesus so that His words, rather than our thoughts, control us. This can only happen when we say "yes" to Him in every room of our lives.

The Spirit Walk, then, is well described by these three ideas:

> **Be completely rooted in the Vine =**
> **Let the wineskin of your mind be**
> **influenced only by the Spirit =**
> **Let Jesus and His word have free**
> **access to every room of your life**

If you are uncomfortable talking about "being filled with the Spirit," remember that it is the same as abiding in Christ. And it is the same as letting the word of Christ fully dwell in you.

We must reshape our cultural misunderstanding of the Spirit Walk. When someone uses the term "being filled with the Spirit" and is only referring to sensational experiences, they are misusing, and ultimately misunderstanding, this term. It is our responsibility to offer gentle reminders to those who incorrectly use this term that it is intended to refer to experiences that affect your daily walk. The Spirit Walk is a 24-7 lifestyle. Only when we speak up can we hope to shift the cultural misconception about this life-giving concept.

Keeping in Step with the Spirit

The Spirit Walk is an ongoing relationship with the Holy Spirit. The goal of this relationship is not a one-time experience, but a daily life in which He fills you and guides you in every moment.

The Bible gives an additional clear picture to explain this process: walking down a path with a guide.

> *But I say, walk by the Spirit, and you will not gratify the desires of the flesh. For the desires of the flesh are against the Spirit, and the desires of the Spirit are against the flesh, for these are opposed to each other, to keep you from doing the things you want to do. But if you are led by the Spirit, you are not under the law… If we live by the Spirit, let us also keep in step with the Spirit.* (Gal. 5:16–18, 25)

Freedom!

Imagine that you are striking off through uncharted mountains aiming for a final destination. You've never walked this path, but a famous guide (think Daniel Boone) offers to take you on the several-month journey. He will do so under one condition: you follow his track and keep up with him no matter how treacherous the path may seem. No matter your misgivings, you surrender these to his greater wisdom. He tells you to put your feet exactly where his have been. If you keep in step with this trailblazer, then you will find your way safely to the destination.

Abiding in Christ, being filled with the Spirit, and letting the word of Christ richly dwell in you describe the same experience: walking in step with the Spirit who is the heavenly Guide. This is the Spirit Walk. Your spiritual path is uncharted, but the Spirit will guide you each step if you let Him. One of His names in the original language of the New Testament (*Paraclete;* see John 14:16, 26) simply means "one who comes along side to help." He is your Advocate, Guide, and Helper. He wants to come alongside you and offer the guidance and assistance you need for each circumstance.

Go back to our illustration of the wilderness trailblazer. You have been traveling with him for several days and feel you are getting the hang of trekking the wilderness. Even so, I doubt you will make this mistake: awaken with the sunrise, make coffee around the campfire, question your guide about the path for the day, and then strike off *alone*. That would be foolish.

Yet how often do we do this in regard to abiding in Christ and being led by the Spirit? We feel like we are doing pretty well spending quiet time with God to start each day—at least better than those who do not. We sit down with our mug of coffee, read the Word, invite God into our lives afresh, and ask Him for wisdom and help for the day. But then we *leave* His Lordship and conscious Presence in the quiet time chair and strike off on our own the rest of the day.

Having a quiet time does not mean you are abiding in Christ.

Starting your day with your heavenly Guide[3] does not mean you are being led by Him the rest of the day.

If you will keep the wilderness path

> **HAVING A QUIET TIME DOES NOT MEAN YOU ARE ABIDING IN CHRIST.** STARTING YOUR DAY WITH YOUR HEAVENLY GUIDE DOES NOT MEAN YOU ARE BEING LED BY HIM THE REST OF THE DAY.

metaphor in the forefront of your mind, then this will help you understand the meaning of being led by the Spirit. The only way for the kingdom to come fully to your life and fully around you is by letting the Guide take you forward step by step.

Galatians 5:25 says we *live* by the Spirit. In other words, our new spiritual lives are birthed by the Spirit of God. He is the One who made us new creations. The Spirit of God takes up residence in us. We never doubt this.

But the question is whether we keep in step with His leadership.

> *If we live by the Spirit, let us also keep in*
> *step with the Spirit.* (Gal. 5:25)

Jesus promises never to leave you but that does not automatically mean He is leading in your life.

---

3 Let's not let the New Age movement's emphasis on having a "spiritual guide" (which is not referring to the God of the Bible) rob us of recognizing the Spirit of God as *our* true heavenly Guide.

Return to our wilderness trek. Can you imagine leaving the wilderness campfire, hundreds of miles from any known landmark, and striking off on your own into territory you have never seen? Imagine the guide following behind you rather than you behind him. Though he does not desert you, he allows you to make your own choices. You may choose the wrong path and he strongly urges you not to do so. Yet the choice is ultimately yours.

At this point, who is in the lead? You are, not the guide.

When it comes to your spiritual walk, who are you truly being led by each day?

In the Spirit Walk, God leads. We follow. Not the other way around.

We must learn to keep in step with the way that He leads.

The Fruit Becomes Effortless

But the fruit of the Spirit is love, joy, peace, patience, kindness, goodness, faithfulness, gentleness, self-control; against such things there is no law. (Gal. 5:22–23)

Frequently, we pursue the fruit of the Spirit: love, joy, peace, patience, kindness, goodness, faithfulness, gentleness, and self-control.

We want more love, more joy, more peace, more self-control.

We pursue the fruit but ignore the source of the fruit.

How can we bear the fruit without starting with the source?

How can you bear fruit without the plant that produces it? The fruit of the Spirit are the result of the Holy Spirit's control of your life. If you want the fruit, you must want the source. Pursuing the fruit without the source is *fruitless* and frustrating.

When you let the Spirit fill you, the fruit naturally emerges in your life.

If you want to be more *loving*, then be full of the Spirit.

If you want to be more *patient*, then be full of the Spirit.

Learn daily to crucify yourself and let Christ fully dwell in you. Then you will produce all the fruit of love, joy, peace, patience, kindness, goodness, faithfulness, gentleness, and self-control.

Over the course of several weeks, I taught fellow missionaries in Southeast Asia about being full of the Spirit. One day I received a short email from one of them. It simply said, "I've really enjoyed this series, it has changed me. Thanks!"

When I asked this missionary what had helped, he responded with these words:

It was the concise nature in the way you presented the information.

I've heard, done, and experienced all of the elements before and have had short times of being filled but it never lasted long. It was always elusive and mysterious. So many pastors just throw it out there—"be filled with the Spirit"—but give no real guidance on how to do it. Not that it is a 3-step process but there are critical components.

*Now that I have experienced being filled for a longer period of time, I truly understand that the fruit of the Spirit (Love, Joy, Peace...) becomes **effortless to execute** since He is doing it and it is not from my flesh. I've spent many years trying to have the fruit of the Spirit through the power of my own effort. To be sure, I asked God for help to exhibit the fruit but I was not S.W.A.P.ing [the process described in this book], not giving it all. Working for the result (the fruit) but not the cause (being filled).*

I think really the "A" ["avoid sin"] was the big one for me and the way you related it to marriage. It helped give me a concrete example. It is really impossible to take something away without filling the hole with something else. Now I understand what I am missing out on when I trivialize and even just entertain the temptation. I think when we are entertaining the temptation, we have already offended God and have already sinned. I know what it is like to offend my wife, which has now helped me to understand what it means to offend God.

No one is exempt from the risk of blocking the Holy Spirit from certain parts of their being. Even missionaries can "serve God" and not be full of the Spirit. Missionaries are normal believers just like anyone else. They, too, must learn to surrender daily to the leadership of the Holy Spirit.

The Dance

I'm not much of a dancer. The few times I have tried taking my wife in my arms and moving in time with the music, I have been stymied by the dance steps. I am supposed to lead and she's supposed to follow. But it doesn't matter if I am leading or she is—keeping in step with each other is not second nature yet. If I were really committed to it and practiced a lot, it could become second nature—maybe.

The Holy Spirit wants to lead you through the dance of life each day. He is the One leading and you must keep in step with Him. It may not be second nature yet, but with practice, it will be. One day, you will simply hear His voice, feel His leading, and keep right in step with Him.

I invite you to explore the Scriptures to learn how to walk in step with the Spirit hour by hour. Learn the spiritual dance. After all, the dance is what you were created for—communing hour by hour with your Maker, completely dependent on Him

To make the most of this journey, you must do two things:

First, you must surrender your heart and mind to whatever the Bible reveals. Let the word of Christ dwell in you richly as you study this subject.

Second, you will need to take time away with God to let Him work on your heart in the same way that He has through the saints throughout the centuries.

Knowing the steps of the Spirit Walk, described by the S.W.A.P. acronym, is indispensable. But this book can only point you to those steps. You must do the hard work of letting God work on your heart afresh.

> *But the hour is coming, and is now here, when the true worshipers will worship the Father in spirit and truth,* **for the Father is seeking such people** *to worship him. God is spirit, and those who worship him must worship in spirit and truth.* (John 4:23–24, emphasis added)

The good news is that the Lord of the dance is waiting for you. He is tapping you on the shoulder and wants this dance. He has wanted it since before the foundation of time. Call it a dance. Call it the Spirit Walk. Regardless, the invitation is for you.

Questions to Ponder

1. How does thinking about the Holy Spirit as the Spirit of Jesus help you as you think about the Spirit Walk?

2. Abiding in Christ, being filled with the Spirit, letting the word of Christ richly dwell within us, keeping in step with the Spirit: how does each nuance of describing the same process help you understand the Spirit Walk?
3. How well have you been doing letting the holy Trailblazer guide you on the journey? What changes would you like to make?
4. The Lord of the dance is inviting you to walk in step with Him. Take time now to invite Him to teach you the steps. Surrender to Him as your King.

CHAPTER 3

S.W.A.P YOUR CONTROL FOR GOD'S

The Spirit Walk is unpredictable. But the process of learning the steps of walking in the Spirit of God *is* predictable. The Bible and its application throughout history point to common patterns that we must follow. They are the spiritual disciplines of learning to let the Spirit guide us every day.

Marriage: The Closest Earthly Picture of This Relationship

The Holy Spirit is a person. The strongest picture of His relationship with us is marriage. God jealously yearns over the Spirit He has put in us. In Christ, God has married us and wants an *exclusive* relationship with us. He wants us to be faithful to Him, not "'til death do us part," but for all of eternity.

Paul uses this picture in Ephesians 5 to describe the mysterious nature of our relationship with God. The picture first applies to the relationship of Christ with His Church (all believers around the world) but can be extended down to His individual relationship with each of us.

> *Wives, submit to your own husbands, as to the Lord. For the husband is the head of the wife even as Christ is the head of the church, his body, and is himself its Savior. Now as the church submits to Christ, so also wives should submit in everything to their husbands.*
>
> *Husbands, love your wives, as Christ loved the church and gave himself up for her, that he might sanctify her, having cleansed her by the washing of water with the word, so that he might present the church to himself in splendor, without spot or wrinkle or any such thing, that she might be holy and without blemish. In the same way husbands should love their wives as their own bodies. He who loves his wife loves himself. For no one ever hated his own flesh, but nourishes and cherishes it, just as Christ does the church, because we are members of his body. "Therefore a man shall leave his father and mother and hold fast to his wife, and the two shall become one flesh." **This mystery is profound, and I am saying that it refers to Christ and the church**. However, let each one of you love his wife as himself, and let the wife see that she respects her husband.* (Eph. 5:22–33, emphasis added)

Whether you are married or not, you have in your mind a picture of the ideal marriage. Walking in step with the Spirit is illustrated by marriage. If you think of your relationship with the Holy Spirit as a relationship with someone you have married, you will learn how to keep in step and live in harmony with Him.

Since the Holy Spirit is a person, as a believer you can be in a good relationship or a bad relationship with Him. But the relationship (marriage) is still there. The Spirit of God is married to you and promises never to abandon you.

But a marriage itself does not become a *good* marriage on its own. Good marriages take work. Period. A good relationship with the Spirit takes the same kind of work.

> **"** BUT A MARRIAGE ITSELF DOES NOT BECOME A GOOD MARRIAGE ON ITS OWN. **GOOD MARRIAGES TAKE WORK. PERIOD.** A GOOD RELATIONSHIP WITH THE SPIRIT TAKES THE SAME KIND OF WORK. **"**

Being married to the Spirit is a lot like learning to live in a beautiful, harmonious relationship with someone here on earth. Because the Holy Spirit is a person, you can offend Him and grieve Him (Eph. 4:30). The relationship can become strained, though it cannot end. The Holy Spirit will not divorce you, but your marriage can certainly become uncomfortable.

The most uncomfortable spiritual marriages are when believers live for themselves, ignoring the conviction of the Spirit. His words gnaw, nag, and hound them, but they ignore Him, ignore His power, ignore His guidance. It is a hellish marriage. The enemy, Satan, is really the one calling the shots and wrecking their relationship. He steals, kills, and destroys when he reigns in your life.

The thief comes only to steal and kill and destroy. I came that they may have life and have it abundantly. (John 10:10)

Making yourself a friend of the world and allowing the adversary to rule you makes you an enemy of God (James 4:4). You can start your day with God in your quiet time, but if you take back control, you are befriending the world. If you are involved in the wrong relationships, are unkind to others, speak belittling words, or let your thoughts run rampant, you show that you are actually more controlled by the enemy than by God. This does not make for a healthy marriage to God.

Who do you think will win in the end? In this spiritual marriage, Jesus Christ is the head of the household, not you. Learn to submit to His leadership in the marriage. Then it will be a happy one.

In Ephesians 5, Paul describes what marriages *should* look like. Husbands loving their wives unconditionally, laying down their lives sacrificially as Christ did for the church. Wives respecting, submitting to, and following the leadership of their husbands as the church does to Jesus. Paul teaches husbands and wives to learn from Christ and His relationship with His church.

But then he goes a step further, explaining that the mystery of this metaphor is great.

This mystery is profound, and I am saying that it refers to Christ and the church. (Eph. 5:32)

On the surface, he is referring to earthly marriage. But in fact, he is really talking about a much deeper relationship—an eternal one—our relationship with Jesus. To understand not only the picture of Christ and the church, but the picture of the Holy Spirit and the disciple, we must remember the picture of marriage. It is the closest earthly picture of what it is like to walk with the Spirit of God on a daily basis.

As we continue this discussion, I will come back the analogy of a marriage to illustrate how to apply the truth of the Scripture to the Spirit Walk. Whether you are single or married, whether you are in a good marriage or a difficult one, let the picture of an ideal marriage inspire you in your walk with God.

The marriage analogy can only be pressed so far. But it will serve us well as we explore the predictable steps we should take for the unpredictable path led by the Spirit.

S.W.A.P. Your Control for His Control

The crux of walking in the Spirit is who is in control and how well that control is working in your life. When you allow the Lord to be in control of your life and to be the One guiding you every minute of the day, that is called being full of the Spirit.

Every day, every moment, someone or something controls you. How can you swap out your own personal control for the control of God in your life? Daily, you need to make a swap: giving up your control and surrendering to His.

> **EVERY DAY, EVERY MOMENT, SOMEONE OR SOMETHING CONTROLS YOU.** HOW CAN YOU SWAP OUT YOUR OWN PERSONAL CONTROL FOR THE CONTROL OF GOD IN YOUR LIFE?

This brings us back to the acronym that summarizes the four broad areas that the Bible gives for walking in the Spirit.

Surrender to His will and His every word
Wait on God in prayer
Avoid sin and let God root out all unrighteousness
Pursue the promptings of the spirit

All over the world, S.W.A.P. is helping ordinary believers learn how to live in an extraordinary way in a broken world. It describes a process to return to the ancient ways of the Spirit Walk. The chapters that follow will help you understand how to assume each of these postures in practical ways. S.W.A.P. describes a deep overall process, but because it can be remembered clearly, you can more easily exercise these disciplines. My hope is that you can then increasingly assume the Spirit Walk over the "self walk."

Remember that S.W.A.P. is not *sequential*. These are not four ordered steps in a process. Rather, the first three happen simultaneously and lead to the final discipline of pursuing the promptings of the Spirit. But each of these concepts is deep enough to require separate chapters to illustrate the spiritual nuances.

On most days in my daily devotional time, I try to go through the S.W.A.P. process to make sure I am set up to walk in the Spirit that day. Throughout the day, I often recall the S.W.A.P. acronym to ensure that I am still walking in the Spirit. S.W.A.P. is just one simple way to describe what the Bible describes. You can use this acronym to kickstart your walk with the Spirit and to hold yourself accountable each and every day.

Two Applications of S.W.A.P.

S.W.A.P. will take on two broad applications in your life. These two applications become vital in the next steps of your journey. In the beginning, you may have to go through the S.W.A.P. process over a period of several days to be filled with the Spirit afresh. God may have many things that He wants to work through in your heart before He reasserts full control over you. You need deep, life-changing periods of swapping your control for His.

But after being filled with the Spirit, He wants to engage in the S.W.A.P. process with you each day to make sure that you are staying fresh in Him and listening to His voice. Daily, you must swap your control for His.

Let's Start the Journey

Let's be clear about one thing: the Spirit Walk is not a 3-step process, but is a living journey with the Creator of the Universe. Just as we would not entitle a book "4 Steps to a Happy Marriage," so this book is not entitled "4 Steps to Being Filled with the Spirit."

Remember with whom you are dealing: the Holy Spirit of the Almighty God!

We do not dictate to Him.

We do not hand Him a timetable.

We are on His agenda and on His schedule.

Where He takes you is unpredictable, but the path toward that interaction is predictable. God earnestly desires for His Spirit to dwell in you fully. Therefore, He wants you to understand the divine process for walking with Him.

S.W.A.P. only intends to outline and help you understand what the Bible explains about walking in the Spirit, or letting Him lead the relationship. It is simply *one* way to help you remember what the Bible teaches so that you can implement this in your life.

You have a choice in this marriage. You can surrender to God so that it becomes an intimate one or allow it to become a strained one. You can attempt to be in control—to play the role of the husband. You can try to do something only He can do—lead the marriage. Marital disharmony awaits.

Or you can S.W.A.P. roles. Let Him lead and you submit. Let Him demonstrate His sacrificial loving Lordship while you respond with respect, worship, and adoration.

The Spirit Walk is not just a journey on a sailboat with the Wind of the Spirit blowing.

It is not just a trek through the mountains led by a heavenly Guide.

It is an invitation to the sweetest relationship imaginable—what every marriage was meant to picture. It's the wedded bliss you were designed for.

Launch the sailboat.

Set the camp.

Start the honeymoon.

S.W.A.P. your control for His! You will never be disappointed that you did.

Questions to Ponder

1. Why is it helpful to think about your relationship with the Spirit as a perfect marriage?
2. What have you learned in marriage, or in the marriages of others, that might help you as you think about developing a daily relationship with the Holy Spirit?
3. If you really want a good "marriage" with the Holy Spirit, how willing are you to work on your part as

a partner? Are you willing to make the changes in your relationship that He reveals to you?

4. S.W.A.P. describes four biblical activities that help you build a better marriage with the Spirit. Recite these four activities and explain what you best understand them to mean at this point.

5. How hungry are you for God and His control over your life? If you are not feeling hungry, are you willing to be hungry? Share with your group of intrepid friends any fears you may have.

6. Ask God now to create a deep hunger for Him and for you to do your part to create the ideal spiritual marriage.

CHAPTER 4

S.W.A.P. – SURRENDER TO HIS WILL AND WORD

As we start the Spirit Walk, we must understand what *God* says about how to be filled the Spirit. It is easy to let our own perceptions sway the path forward. Too often, stories and anecdotes build our theology of the Spirit rather than the clear teaching of the Bible. Many practical frameworks detailing "how to walk in the Spirit" are built only on the stories of the Bible and not the clear teachings of the Bible; they are built upon experiences and testimonies rather than biblical principles.

S.W.A.P. attempts to start with the clear teachings of the Bible and then to allow the examples and stories from the Bible to illustrate what those mean. S.W.A.P. is a framework, or skeletal structure, to support the teaching of the Bible. Just like your skeleton is the foundation for building muscles, enclosing vital organs and supporting the part of you we see on the outside, S.W.A.P. is meant to provide the foundation and support for your Spirit Walk. It simply acts as the biblical skeletal structure upon which you build your relationship with the Holy Spirit. The part of you we see on the outside—the fruit of the Spirit in your life, the gifts of the Spirit in your life, the fruit of your ministry—are all built upon these foundational principles.

Surrender to His will and His every word
Wait on God in prayer
Avoid sin and let God root out all unrighteousness
Pursue the promptings of the Spirit

This chapter and the ones that follow will explain this biblical framework in depth. Let's start with the first: SURRENDER.

Building a Proper Framework

A biblical framework for any area of life or theology is built upon the commands of Scripture first, general principles second, and illustrations of the lives of people third.

For example, our relationships with people are not always simple. And sometimes, we will cross paths with people who disappoint us, betray us or even harm us. But the biblical framework for loving our enemies is right in front of our eyes, and it's built this way:

> *"You have heard that it was said, 'You shall love your neighbor and hate your enemy.' But I say to you, Love your enemies and pray for those who persecute you, so that you may be sons of your Father who is in heaven. For he makes his sun rise on the evil and on the good, and sends rain on the just and on the*

unjust. For if you love those who love you, what reward do you have? Do not even the tax collectors do the same? And if you greet only your brothers, what more are you doing than others? Do not even the Gentiles do the same? You therefore must be perfect, as your heavenly Father is perfect." (Matt. 5:43–48)

In trying to understand how to respond to enemies, *a framework should start with commands.* The clear commands from Jesus are in Matthew 5:44, "Love your enemies and pray for those who persecute you." In Luke 6:27–28, He adds, "Do good to those who hate you, bless those who curse you." The framework starts with these key takeaways: love, pray for, do good to, and bless your enemies.

Second, we look for principles to further expand our understanding and framework. Here is one example:

Beloved, never avenge yourselves, but leave it to the wrath of God, for it is written, "Vengeance is mine, I will repay, says the Lord." To the contrary, "if your enemy is hungry, feed him; if he is thirsty, give him something to drink; for by so doing you will heap burning coals on his head." Do not be overcome by evil, but overcome evil with good. (Rom. 12:19–21)

Now add to our framework the principle of the sovereignty of a good God. It is *God's* job to avenge, not ours. He is our Protector. We must trust Him. That is why we bless rather than take revenge. In the very act of doing good to our enemies, we heap burning coals on their heads.

It shames their actions and allows room for God to demonstrate His power in us. In loving our enemies, we then overcome evil with good. Now we have a clear principle: God is the avenger and will take care of us; loving enemies demonstrates God's power in us; victory comes through doing good, not evil, when we are mistreated.

Finally, we look for examples in the Bible to show us how to do this. Here are two:

1. Jesus, on trial, refused to curse back when cursed by the guards. On the cross, He asked His Father to forgive His persecutors rather than strike them down. The declaration of the centurion was, "Surely this was the Son of God!"
2. Stephen, the first martyr, followed the example of Jesus and asked God not to hold his persecutors' sins against them. A young man named Saul saw this demonstration of God's power. It would later impact his life.

This is how biblical frameworks are built.

Four Commands in the S.W.A.P. Framework

*Abide in me, and I in you.... If you **abide in me, and my words abide in you**, ask whatever you wish, and it will be done for you.... As the Father has loved me, so have I loved you.*

*Abide in my love. If you **keep my commandments**, you will abide in my love, just as I have kept my Father's commandments and abide in his love.* (John 15:4, 7, 9–10, emphasis added)

*And do not get drunk with wine, for that is debauchery, but **be filled with the Spirit**.* (Eph. 5:18, emphasis added)

***Let the word of Christ dwell in you richly**, teaching and admonishing one another in all wisdom, singing psalms and hymns and spiritual songs, with thankfulness in your hearts to God.* (Col. 3:16, emphasis added)

*But I say, **walk by the Spirit**, and you will not gratify the desires of the flesh. If we live by the Spirit, let us also **keep in step with the Spirit**.* (Gal. 5:16, 25, emphasis added)

Among the clear commands and descriptions about walking in the Spirit, it is helpful to highlight the four above, which we have already referred to:

1. Be **rooted** completely **in the vine** so that the sap of His Word flows through you.
2. Let the **wineskin** of your mind **be filled** and influenced only by the Spirit.
3. Let Jesus and His word have **unhindered access to every room** of your life.
4. **Keep in step** with the heavenly **Guide**.

These four commands describe the same process. Each shouts one word, which describes the first activity in our framework: CONTROL! The essential question is whether you are letting God control and fill you in each moment. To be filled is to be controlled. If you are filled with alcohol, you are controlled by its influence. If you drive your car that way, you will get arrested. That is how powerful the influence of

> **"** ARE YOU SO FILLED WITH THE SPIRIT THAT YOU COULD BE RECOGNIZED AS **"UNDER HIS INFLUENCE"**? **"**

a substance can be. Are you so filled with the Spirit that you could be recognized as "under His influence"?

The way God fills us is through the third person of the Trinity: the Holy Spirit. God the Father is on His throne in heaven. Jesus, the Son, intercedes for us at His right hand. But both become present with us through the person of the Spirit. This is His role.

The images associated with each command above contribute their own nuances to the process of being filled with the Spirit.

1. A branch only has life as it stays connected to the vine. The vine controls it.
2. A wineskin's function is to let the wine (and no other substance) fill it to the brim.
3. The home of a heart is only owned by the landlord if he has the key to every room.

4. Your path through the wilderness only works if the guide has complete authority on where and how you will trek.

It all comes back to control. Being controlled by the Spirit leads to the first posture of the S.W.A.P. framework: **Surrender**.

Surrender, Not Commitment

The essence of control is surrender. And surrender is not the same as commitment.

THE ESSENCE OF CONTROL IS SURRENDER. AND SURRENDER IS NOT THE SAME AS COMMITMENT.

The late pastor Dr. Adrian Rogers told of a conversation with a Romanian pastor, Josef Tson, who suffered during the Communist reign in his country. Dr. Rogers asked Josef of his impression of American Christianity. With some reluctance, Josef shared his impressions:

> "The key word in American Christianity is *commitment*.... The word *commitment* did not come into great usage in the English language until about the 1960s. In Romania we do not even have a word to translate the English word *commitment*. If you were to use *commitment* in your message tonight, I would not have a proper word to translate it with."

> Josef continued, "When a new word comes into usage, it generally pushes an old word out. I

began to study and found the old word that *commitment* replaced. Adrian, the old word that is no longer in vogue in America is the word *surrender*."

"Josef," I asked, "*what* is the difference between *commitment* and *surrender*?"

He said, "When you make a commitment, you are still in control, no matter how noble the thing you commit to. One can commit to pray, to study the Bible, to give money, or to commit to automobile payments, or to lose weight. Whatever he chooses to do, he *commits* to it. But *surrender* is different. If someone holds a gun and asks you to lift your hands in the air as a token of surrender, you don't tell that person what you are committed to. You simply surrender and do as you are told."

He said, "Americans love commitment because they are still in control. But the key word is *surrender*. We are to be slaves of the Lord Jesus Christ."[4]

Commitment can be self-centered and cause-centered. Commitment is fundamentally about "me." How strongly am *I* devoted to someone or something? Surrender is all about the other person. I relinquish my rights and give up control to someone or something else.

---

4 Adrian Rogers, *The Incredible Power of Kingdom Authority* (Nashville: B&H, 2002), 60–61.

Our churches are filled with nominally committed churchgoers who have "prayed the prayer" and show up at services occasionally. Scattered among them are a few committed Christians who show up regularly, are earnest in their faith, and do most of the work.

But how many *surrendered* disciples do we have—disciples completely sold out to Jesus and His agenda for their lives? Commitment is not a bad thing, except when it gets in the way of surrender.

> COMMITMENT IS NOT A BAD THING, EXCEPT WHEN IT GETS IN THE WAY OF SURRENDER.

"Committed to Me or to a Task?"

When my wife and I were church planters in Los Angeles in the early days of our marriage, the Lord clearly told us to move to the inner city to start a church. We landed in a gang-infested, crime-ridden neighborhood. The first evening, my car windshield was shattered. The first week, a person was gunned down in the apartment building next door in a drive-by shooting. It took a lot of work to keep us in the place of surrender.

Part of that surrender was a twenty-year commitment to start and shepherd that church. After eight years, God began stirring my heart that it was time for us to move from church planting in the States to multiplying churches in unreached nations.

For months, in my daily quiet times, my soul was restless. Was this the voice of God or a distraction? For a long time, I blocked out this voice. It couldn't be God, could it? We had a twenty-year agreement and, with gritted teeth, I was committed to the task.

One day, God's voice broke through my thoughts, piercing my soul. "Steve, are you committed to Me or to a task?" In that moment, I realized that I was no longer surrendered—only committed. I was living in a past word of God, not the latest word of God.

God acted in a similar way with Abraham, the man of faith (Heb. 11:17–19). He told Abraham to sacrifice his son, Isaac. As hard as it was, Abraham listened (Gen. 22:2) and obeyed. Undoubtedly, this was a test of Abraham's faith, surrender, and commitment. As Abraham climbed the mountain with Isaac and the stack of wood on his son's back, he kept listening to the voice of God. As he laid his son on the altar and bound him, he kept listening. He stayed committed to each fresh word because of the surrender of his heart. As he raised his knife to slay his only son, he kept listening (Gen. 22:11).

God cried out and His servant obeyed. The knife dropped from his hand and he unbound his son.

Surrender.

How tragic if Abraham had acted on the first word of God only but stopped listening!

Surrender.

And God changed the sacrifice from Abraham's son to a ram (Gen 22:13). How like God! How good He is!

Commitment is a good thing when it marches us from the point of surrender, with gritted teeth and hearts full of faith, toward God's plan. For it to be surrendered commitment, however, our ears must continually listen for His voice to guide, turn, and direct us along the journey.

How easy for us to live committed to a word God spoke years earlier. It is a noble thing to stay committed to that....until God gives a fresh word.

> *Who among you fears the LORD*
> *and obeys the voice of his servant?*
> *Let him who walks in darkness*
> *and has no light*
> *trust in the name of the LORD*
> *and rely on his God.*
> *Behold, all you who kindle a fire,*
> *who equip yourselves with burning torches!*
> *Walk by the light of your fire,*
> *and by the torches that you have kindled!*
> *This you have from my hand:*
> *you shall lie down in torment.* (Isa. 50:10–11)

God warns us to keep walking forward in times of darkness. We must be careful not to kindle our own fires and come up with human thoughts that allow us to escape what God has clearly spoken. Commitment to the words God speaks is a stabilizing force.

On the other hand, when God *does* speak afresh, we must be ready to say "yes" just as quickly as Abraham did. Otherwise, our lives dissolve into agendas and plans shaped by what we *think* God wants us to do, which we later ask God to bless. That is not surrender.

The Blank Paper of Surrender

Surrender is like this: In your morning quiet time, God prompts you to take out a blank sheet of paper. With anticipation, you pull it out and grasp your pen. You are ready to write, for God is speaking. Next, He says, "My child, this is the contract for the day. Sign the contract at the bottom of the page." You look at the blank sheet. Nervously you respond, "Okay, Father, I will sign it. But what are the terms of the contract? The page is blank. Fill it out so I can sign it." Your Father pauses, and then His gentle voice says, "My child, I will not tell you ahead of time. Just sign it, and then I will fill in the details."

Total surrender does not include negotiations. If you sign that blank paper, you are surrendering to God. But if you wait for God to write the terms of the contract, adjust it with your negotiations, and then sign it conditionally, the focus is still on yourself. By making even subtle changes, you are moving closer to commitment and further from surrender.

Only commanders surrendering on the battlefield sign blank sheets of paper. The terms are unconditional. Their surrender is total.

God wants you to sign the blank paper of surrender daily. You cannot be filled with the Spirit until you are emptied of yourself—your will, primarily. To fill a wineskin or a bottle with wine, you must empty the current contents. You must pour everything onto the ground and let the container be filled afresh.

Are you willing to let God empty you of your own control?

The trailhead of walking in the Spirit is marked with a sign: "Surrender." It is the hardest place to start. But it is the *only* place to start.

Can You Trust God?

Why is it so hard? Because of the nature of surrender. We are giving up our will for God's will. We are reluctant to surrender to God's will because, at the core of our being, we do not trust that God is good.

Perhaps we believe that He is good in the sense of good (righteous) versus evil. But do we trust that He is good in terms of being a loving, benevolent Father to us?

For eleven years as a Christian I struggled with the goodness of God. For eleven years, I did not know the joy of the fullness of the Spirit. I was still in control. I had not completely surrendered. The underlying reason? I believed I knew what was best for my life. I had plans for my happiness and fulfillment. I mistrusted God. I sensed that if I said "yes" to God, He would call me to do things that brought misery to my life.

After a period of fasting, praying, and poring over my Bible, I came to the realization that this Father, this loving Creator, knew *me*. He had fashioned every cell in my body.

> *For you formed my inward parts;*
> *you knitted me together in my mother's womb.*
> *I praise you, for I am fearfully and wonderfully made.*
> *Wonderful are your works;*
> *my soul knows it very well.*
> *My frame was not hidden from you,*
> *when I was being made in secret,*
> *intricately woven in the depths of the earth.*
> *Your eyes saw my unformed substance;*
> *in your book were written, every one of them,*
> *the days that were formed for me,*
> *when as yet there was none of them.* (Ps. 139:13–16)

If He created me and were a benevolent Father, couldn't He design the days and plans for my life that would fill me with pleasure while bringing the greatest glory to Himself? When I settled God's goodness in my heart, knowing that His plans would bring the greatest fulfillment, I ran to His arms. I surrendered myself completely to Him. For the first time in my life I was conscious of being completely filled with the Spirit. In my surrender, I was finally free and full of joy.

> *In your presence there is fullness of joy;*
> *at your right hand are pleasures forevermore.* (Ps. 16:11)

God is good. It is a *loving* goodness. He fashioned every cell in your body. Surrendering to Him is not only for His glory, but is for your joy, pleasure, and fulfillment. Only God, your Creator, knows how to blaze a path for your life that brings both Him and you the greatest pleasure.

Prior to settling in to the Spirit Walk, you must settle the theology of God's goodness.

You can trust your Father. He is good. Until you believe that, you will not surrender. Even when you do believe, it is easy to forget God's goodness as life goes on. At key junctures in life, you pull back from surrender because you again assume you know best. You must continually remember that God always knows best. And His will, no matter how painful, will bring the greatest fulfillment and fruit in the end.

> *He [Jesus] said to them, "I have food to eat that you do not know about.... My food is to do the will of him who sent me and to accomplish his work." (John 4:32, 34)*

Surrender to God's will and to His work is true, nourishing food.

Surrender to His Will

> *And do not get drunk with wine, for that is debauchery, but be filled with the Spirit. (Eph. 5:18)*

Let the word of Christ dwell in you richly, teaching and admonishing one another in all wisdom, singing psalms and hymns and spiritual songs, with thankfulness in your hearts to God. (Col. 3:16)

Surrender demonstrates itself in two areas—the will of God and the words of God. The Ephesians passage above describes absolute surrender to the will of the Spirit wherever He takes us. Like Jesus in the garden of Gethsemane, we pray:

"Nevertheless, not my will, but yours, be done." (Luke 22:42)

The Colossians passage above describes not only being committed to the will of God, but letting each daily—even hourly—word that Christ speaks to us reign. We are surrendered to each word that we encounter.

The fullness of the Spirit starts at this trailhead: "Surrender to His will."

The filling of the wineskin begins with this act: emptying yourself of your control.

The occupying of the house commences with this greeting: "Lord, here are all of the keys."

Abiding in Christ is initiated with your signature on a blank sheet of paper.

ABIDING IN CHRIST IS INITIATED WITH **YOUR SIGNATURE ON A BLANK SHEET OF PAPER**.

Unconditional surrender is a joyful enterprise when you trust that God has your welfare at heart.

The Great Commission Promise

One reason the church lacks the visible presence of God and why revival eludes us is our refusal to surrender to the absolute will of God. Our church agenda and prosperity too often trump surrender to the King and His reign in this earth. We fail to get church right because we fail to get the kingdom right first. At the center of the kingdom of God is the King. Yet, too often, our churches have at their center a half-hearted surrender to the King. What is best for our church nearly always overrides what is best for the King's reign.

For example, we may think our church is mission minded. But too often giving financially to support the Great Commission pales in comparison to dedicating funds to church socials, building and renovation projects, equipment for the Sunday morning main event, and so on.

Surrendering our church agenda to the King might look more like this: The church I attend—WoodsEdge Community Church, quite a large church—dedicates at least fifty percent of its offerings to ministries and missions outside the walls. Even in contemplating doing some building in the future, they are committed to maintaining this ratio—spending more on missions than their facility and salaries.

Is your church surrendered to the kingship of God or is it more guided by what will best grow and prosper your church?

One barometer of this is surrender to the greatest mission Jesus gave His church.

> *And Jesus came and said to them, "All authority in heaven and on earth has been given to me. Go therefore and make disciples of all nations, baptizing them in the name of the Father and of the Son and of the Holy Spirit, teaching them to observe all that I have commanded you. And behold, I am with you always, to the end of the age."* (Matt. 28:18–20)

Most of us know the Great Commission. We quote it from memory, especially the promise, "I am with you always, to the end of the age." But do you realize that the promise of Jesus's presence is *conditional*? This is not referring to the indwelling presence of the Holy Spirit that never leaves us.

The presence Jesus is describing in the Great Commission is His special presence for the mission. Jesus is sending his disciples upon the core mission on His heart—to take the message of the good news to every people group and place on Earth. He knows it will be difficult, and He promises to accompany His disciples in power. When churches surrender to that mission above their own agendas, they will begin to encounter the presence of Jesus like they never have before.

When the early church was tempted to pull back from the mission when persecution arose, they surrendered afresh to the mission. They did not ask for protection but for God's presence. God honored that request in power because it honored the mission on His heart:

> *"And now, Lord, look upon their threats and grant to your ser-vants to continue to speak your word with all boldness, while you stretch out your hand to heal, and signs and wonders are per-formed through the name of your holy servant Jesus." And when they had prayed, the place in which they were gathered together was shaken, and they were all filled with the Holy Spirit and con-tinued to speak the word of God with boldness.* (Acts 4:29–31)

This was a group of disciples who had already been filled with the Spirit in Acts 2 (on the Day of Pentecost). As they surrendered again to the mission of God, the Spirit filled them anew.

We fail to experience the powerful presence of the Spirit of Jesus because we fail to live according to His will. His will is that His name and His kingdom would become great in every unreached place on earth. When we priori-tize what is best for ourselves and for the welfare of our churches rather than the salvation of the world, is it surpris-ing that revival eludes us?

Make no mistake: living for the mission of God is the most challenging and faith-stretching venture you will ever embark on. Making God's Name great among the nations is costly. Even our Lord was troubled in His spirit as he contemplated the cost of making the Father's name great around the world.

> *"Now is my soul troubled. And what shall I say? 'Father, save me from this hour'? But for this purpose I have come to this hour. **Father, glorify your name." Then a voice came from heaven: "I have glorified it, and I will glorify it again."** The crowd that stood there and heard it said that it had thundered. Others said, "An angel has spoken to him." Jesus answered, "This voice has come for your sake, not mine. Now is the judgment of this world; now will the ruler of this world be cast out. And I, when I am lifted up from the earth, will draw all people to myself." He said this to show by what kind of death he was going to die.* (John 12:27–33)

As Jesus surrendered Himself to the mission—the glory of God in all places—God's voice thundered from heaven. The presence was palpable.

The cost of the mission for Jesus was the cross. But only in death would He bear much fruit. Jesus illustrated this in the verses leading up to this episode:

> *Truly, truly, I say to you, unless a grain of wheat falls into the earth and dies, it remains alone; but if it dies, it bears much fruit. Whoever loves his life loses it, and whoever hates his life in this world will keep it for eternal life. If anyone serves me, he must follow me; and where I am, there will my servant be also. If anyone serves me, the Father will honor him.* (John 12:24–26)

To truly bear fruit in your life, like Jesus, you must become a grain of wheat that falls to the ground and dies. When you lose your life, you gain it. When you serve Christ, you must be where He is. Where is Christ? His special presence leads His disciples to the edge of darkness to proclaim the Light of the World.

When you serve Christ in this way, the Father welcomes that posture. He comes and makes His home with you (see John 14:21, 23). His presence becomes palpable and visible.

This is why I think God is blessing the great church I attend. Their heartbeat is the mission of God—His kingdom coming to America and every unreached place on earth.

O, disciple of Christ, accept the mission and the privilege of counting the cost. In accepting the mission, you will receive the presence of God in power.

O, church, embrace the mandate of His kingdom coming to every nation. Offer up the sacrifices of your best seeds—people, funds, prayer, efforts—and you will be rewarded with the fullness of the Spirit.

Revival only awaits your surrender to the King and His mission.

This is His will.

Surrender to His Every Word

As you surrender to the will of God, each day He will explain to you the implications of that surrender. While Ephesians 5:18 speaks strongly about surrendering to

His will, completely filled with the Spirit, Colossians 3:16 makes it clear that this is a day-by-day process. It is the way Jesus defined His response when tempted by the devil not to surrender to the Father:

*But he answered, "It is written, 'Man shall not live by bread alone, but by **every word** that comes from the mouth of God.'"* (Matt. 4:4, emphasis added)

Here, the picture of marriage aids our understanding. It is one thing for a man to surrender his will to his wife's welfare. In a decorated chapel, flanked by faithful grooms-men, looking at his wife in all her glory, the man steels himself and says, "I do."

But what happens the next morning when the couple awakens and the bride says, "Honey, will you…?" Reality sinks in: a harmonious marriage takes work. The hus-band was not expecting that request, nor the one later in the day. With each "honey-will-you," the spouse has an opportunity to surrender to every word—every request. Surrendering to every word clarifies what surrendering to her will is. This is where marriages break apart—lack of surrender to each "honey-will-you." Sustained surrender to the Spirit is saying yes to every "honey-will-you" that comes your way.

At that eleven-year mark in my Christian life, I expe-rienced the filling of the Spirit afresh by surrendering to God's will. But then, day by day, each Bible reading con-fronted me with a fresh word to surrender to. Each was a challenge of my ability to surrender; a "honey-will-you" as it were.

Have you ever had that experience? Perhaps at a pivotal juncture of your life, you said "yes" to Jesus. But then one day as you were reading your Bible, you found a command that you did not like—one not comfortable to obey.

To go back to the original framework of how to treat your enemies, perhaps you discovered you were supposed to love them. But pray for them? Really, God? Bless them? Really, God? Can't I just tolerate them? Will you stay surrendered? Each new word you discover in the Bible is a challenge to stay surrendered to the Master.

Walking in the Spirit is not simply the result of a one-time experience in which you surrender to the will of God. Such experiences can be dramatic and emotional.

However, such experiences are just the trailheads. Staying on the path means listening to every whisper of your guide. Walking in the Spirit is staying full of the Spirit—continuing to listen to His whispers. To stay full of the Spirit, you must keep saying "yes" to each new word of Jesus that he speaks to your life.

The Spirit Walk is about becoming more and more surrendered, and thus more Christlike.

To grow into all the fullness of God, you must keep saying "yes" to every word of Christ. You will find these as you dig deep into the Bible and ponder how to lovingly obey each one. Jesus will speak to you in these moments.

Saying yes to each "honey-will-you" leads to lasting abiding in God's presence.

Saying yes to each "honey-will-you" fosters increasing life transformation.

Saying yes to each "honey-will-you" guides you toward completeness in Christ.

Saying yes to each "honey-will-you" results in lasting fruitfulness in you and around you.

A balanced Spirit Walk incorporates both surrender to God's will and to God's words: (1) transforming experiences of surrender such as in Acts 2 (Pentecost) and Acts 4:31 (post-persecution) and (2) daily working out the implications of your salvation through each honey-will-you in God's Word:

> *Therefore, my beloved, as you have always obeyed, so now, not only as in my presence but much more in my absence,* **work out your own salvation with fear and trembling,** *for it is God who works in you, both to will and to work for his good pleasure.* (Phil. 2:12–13, emphasis added)

The effects of transforming, bondage-breaking experiences will not last without the daily work of our surrender to each word.

The daily work of surrender will only find its power through the breakthroughs of transforming experiences of surrender.

> Embrace both: surrender to His will and His every word. Fear not either one, for your Creator is good.

Welcome to the Becoming-Complete Process

> *In the days of his flesh, Jesus offered up prayers and supplications, with loud cries and tears, to him who was able to save him from death, and he was heard because of his reverence. Although he was a son, he learned obedience through what he suffered. **And being made perfect**, he became the source of eternal salvation to all who obey him.* (Heb. 5:7–9, emphasis added)

Jesus modeled for us how to walk through this process of surrender. In the wilderness temptations at the beginning of His ministry and in his prayer in the garden of Gethsemane on the last night of His ministry, Jesus demonstrated complete surrender to the Father's will.

But do you realize He had to consciously surrender to every word of the Father? Though Jesus was *sinless* during His earthly ministry, He was not yet *perfect* in His humanity. Perfection comes when we pass each test successfully and come through on the other side having passed the test—complete in every way.

The word "perfect" (*teleioo*, τελειόω) in Hebrews 5:9 carries the idea of coming to fulfillment or becoming complete or mature. It means that something has finally achieved its complete design, not just that it is sin-free or error-free. It has passed every test perfectly.

Abraham had faith, but his faith became completed, proven, and perfect by his works (James 2:22). In the same way, Jesus became perfect, living up to His intended design, as He surrendered to every word the Father spoke.

Hebrews 5:8 says Jesus *learned* obedience through what He suffered. His life was not easy, but as He said "yes" to each word of His Father, He became complete— *teleioo*. He passed every test and surrendered to every command: the mark of perfection.

In the same way, we must not only surrender in the beginning of our lives, but we only become mature and complete by saying "yes" to each word that God speaks to our hearts. If Jesus had to learn obedience, how much more must we?

Starting this journey means coming to the altar and saying "yes." You must sign the blank sheet of paper and surrender to the will of your Husband.

Staying on the path means saying "yes" to every daily "honey-will-you" of your Lord Jesus.

In this process of surrender, the harmony of the relationship thrives.

Questions to Ponder

1. How is surrender different from commitment? Are you willing to sign the blank paper of surrender?
2. Trusting in the goodness and lovingkindness of God is foundational for surrendering to Him. What

needs to change in your perspective of God's goodness and your willingness to surrender to Him?

3. How well are you surrendered to the will and mission of God? Have you ever unconditionally surrendered yourself to Him—no matter what He says?

4. What challenges do you face in surrendering to every fresh word of Christ—every "honey-will-you"?

5. Take time now to pull out a fresh, blank paper. If it expresses your heart, sign your name at the bottom and tell God, "Father, You love me unconditionally. I trust You to guide my life. I surrender to Your control. Write on here any directions for this week, this month, this year, this life. I am Yours!"

CHAPTER 5

S.**W**.A.P. – <u>W</u>AIT ON GOD IN PRAYER (PART 1)

The first three aspects of the S.W.A.P. framework are *simultaneous*, not *sequential*. They are three parts of the same process that lead to the final step of the framework: pursuing the promptings of the Spirit. They lead us into the Spirit Walk—being led by the Spirit in power.

In the previous chapter, we examined the first element of the biblical framework—surrender to His will and His every word. Surrendering to His will entails coming to the altar and saying "yes." You sign the blank sheet of paper and surrender to the will of your Husband and start down the path with Him. *Staying* on the path then means saying "yes" to every daily "honey-will-you" of your Lord Jesus, submitting to every word of Christ. Periodically, as your love grows cold or your surrender grows old, you will need to come back to the altar to renew your vows.

The surrendering process, especially in its initial standing-at-the-altar stage, can take a while. God wants to do deep work to get your heart to a point of *willingness* to fresh surrender. It takes time—unhurried time.

That's the reason for the next element of the framework: **wait on God in prayer.**

Surrender to His will and His every word
Wait on God in prayer
Avoid sin and let God root out all unrighteousness
Pursue the promptings of the Spirit

The Clear Command: Wait

Remember, building a biblical framework must start with the clear commands of Scripture, not just stories or testimonies. Jesus gave clear commands to His first disciples about how they were to be filled with the Spirit initially. Of course, that command was given to a specific group at a specific time. But the command Jesus gave to them illustrates the process that comes with being filled with the Spirit.

Jesus clearly commanded his disciples to wait until God acted upon them by sending His Spirit.

> *And behold, I am sending the promise of my Father upon you. But **stay** in the city until you are clothed with power from on high."* (Luke 24:49, emphasis added)

> *And while staying with them he ordered them not to depart from Jerusalem, but to **wait for the promise of the Father**, which, he said, "you heard from me; for John baptized with*

> *water, but you will be baptized with the Holy Spirit not*
> *many days from now."* (Acts 1:4–5, emphasis added)

After Jesus's ascension into heaven, 120 disciples (ordinary followers of Jesus, not just the eleven apostles) waited in an upper room for around ten days[5], living in unity and praying fervently.

> *All these with one accord were devoting themselves*
> *to prayer, together with the women and Mary the*
> *mother of Jesus, and his brothers.* (Acts 1:14)

Why did Jesus want them to wait? Why not instantly send His Spirit?

The Bible does not clearly tell us why, but in all likelihood it relates to the first point in the framework: *surrender*. How did the early disciples surrender to Jesus's will and His every word? They waited upon Him in prayer, submitting themselves to whatever He said. Think about how much of His teaching they must have pondered as they waited on Him in prayer.

A clue to this being the reason for waiting is found in the dialogue the disciples had with Jesus just after His

---

5 Pentecost is fifty days after Passover. Jesus was crucified on the Friday before Passover (Friday night and Saturday day). He rose from the dead on Sunday and then appeared to His disciples over a period of forty days (Acts 1:3). After this time He ascended into heaven and His disciples waited in the upper room until Pentecost. Pentecost therefore came around ten days after Jesus's ascension.

command to wait. Let's paraphrase it and break it down in everyday language:

> **Disciples:** "Master, we've waited for three years. Will you finally sit on the throne in Jerusalem as King and build your earthly kingdom now?"
>
> **Jesus:** "Stop focusing on these earthly things related to human kings and kingdoms. That's distracting. Instead, wait for the Spirit to clothe you with power, and then go into the whole world to tell people about Me, following me as your King and spreading a heavenly kingdom" (see Acts 1:6–8).

These disciples had spent three years with Jesus. In that time, they listened to His teaching every day and observed His ministry. For three years, they watched Him break the expectations of the Jews regarding the Messiah becoming an earthly king who would throw off the yoke of Roman occupation.

Yet even with Jesus demonstrating that He was a different type of Messiah, the disciples did not yet understand the nature of King Jesus and His reign—the kingdom of God. Faulty thinking still hounded them. The disciples were surrendered to Jesus, but parts of their old thinking, acting, and planning still needed transforming. The time in the upper room gave them the pause they needed to reflect on Jesus's life and ministry, the Old Testament Scriptures, and the clear commands and teachings Jesus had given them. It was a time for God to do a deep work in them to root out whatever needed to be changed. Until that happened, they were not ready to serve God in power.

At the end of the ten days, it appears that the disciples' hearts were surrendered and ready for a move of the Spirit upon them. When the Spirit came in power, they did *exactly what Jesus commanded*—they witnessed to the multitudes. Their surrender was so strong and the mission so clear that they *stuck to the script* Jesus gave them even when the highest authorities tried to suppress their surrender to the Master and the mission:

> *So they called them and charged them not to speak or teach at all in the name of Jesus. But Peter and John answered them, "Whether it is right in the sight of God to listen to you rather than to God, you must judge, for we cannot but speak of what we have seen and heard." And when they had further threatened them, they let them go, finding no way to punish them, because of the people, for all were praising God for what had happened.* (Acts 4:18–21)

> *And when they had brought them, they set them before the council. And the high priest questioned them, saying, "We strictly charged you not to teach in this name, yet here you have filled Jerusalem with your teaching, and you intend to bring this man's blood upon us." But Peter and the apostles answered, "We must obey God rather than men...." When they had called*

> *in the apostles, they beat them and charged them not to speak
> in the name of Jesus, and let them go. Then they left the pres-
> ence of the council, rejoicing that they were counted worthy
> to suffer dishonor for the name. And every day, in the temple
> and from house to house, they did not cease teaching and
> preaching that the Christ is Jesus.* (Acts 5:27–29, 40–42)

Waiting in prayer allows time for God to work deeply in your heart, to root out any thinking, speaking, and acting that does not align with Him and His purposes in your life. When you allow God the time for a deep work in you, then you *stick to the contract* of life He gives you. Whatever He has written on the blank paper is what you live out—no matter the pressures on you.

In the Bible, followers of Jesus most often became filled with the Spirit after a season of desperate waiting and longing for Him. God wants you to hunger for Him. He is delighted when you earnestly seek Him.

> *But an hour is coming, and now is, when the true worshipers will
> worship the Father in spirit and truth; for such people the Father
> seeks to be His worshipers. God is spirit, and those who worship
> Him must worship in spirit and truth.* (John 4:23–24, NASB)

The Father seeks fervent worshippers who bring glory to Him. To worship Him, He requires you to align your will and your thinking to His. He is not in the business of aligning His will and thinking to yours. He is God and you are not.

To be filled with God, you must come God's way. When your Father in heaven has determined that your heart is aligned and ready, He will descend upon you in power.

He delights to come to you—on His terms.

Wait–You Must Be Acted Upon

Be filled with the Spirit. (Eph. 5:18)

What all this means is you must *wait* for God to act. The Bible makes it clear that you must *be* filled. Being filled with the Spirit is a passive posture. God must act upon you. Remember, Ephesians 5:18 does not say, "Fill yourself with the Spirit."

Today, Paul may have stated the idea of filling this way: "Let God keep on filling you up to the brim with His Spirit." This is how the Ephesian church would have heard Paul's command. Note the phrase "be filled" rather than "fill yourselves." Being filled with the Spirit is a divine process. It is an experience of God acting upon you as He honors the surrender of your heart and pours out His Spirit afresh on you.

Even though this is a passive posture, Paul states Ephesians 5:18 as a *command*. It is a command to let God work on your life afresh with His Spirit. It seems strange to command someone to let God do something. But this command is no different than Jesus commanding His

disciples to wait. The Bible commands you to humble
yourself before God
and wait upon Him.
You are to wait *until*
He acts.

> **THE BIBLE COMMANDS YOU TO HUMBLE YOURSELF BEFORE GOD AND WAIT UPON HIM. YOU ARE TO WAIT UNTIL HE ACTS.**

The command of Ephesians 5:18 is a continuous tense.
It can be translated "be continually filled with the Spirit"
or "be filled with the Spirit over and over again." If it were
meant to be a one-time experience early in one's Christian
life, Paul would have chosen a different tense in the Greek
that emphasizes that.

Remember, at salvation you received the indwelling
Spirit. You do not have to wait for a second experience
to receive the Holy Spirit. At salvation, He sealed you in
Christ (Eph. 1:13–14).

But being indwelt does not mean that the Spirit fills
you and controls you. The point of this book is to help
you understand this basic concept and learn how to let
the Spirit take over control. That familiar phrase—*be filled
with the Spirit*—is intended to happen not just once, but
over and over again.

Jeff Wells, my pastor, says: "Most of us Christians
leak!" In other words, though we may have been filled to
fullness in the past, it is easy to gradually take back control
of our lives. We let the control of the Spirit leak out and
our own control dribble back in.

The command and the examples of the Bible state
that being filled with the Spirit happens again and again

and again throughout your life. When you wait on God in prayer, allowing the indwelling Spirit to fill and control you may be a first-time experience. Or it may be the hundredth time you have been filled to the brim with the Spirit.

Though being filled with the Spirit is not a one-time experience, it *is* still an experience. God wants to come upon you in power in a holy and precious moment. That moment is sweeter for coming after a period of waiting, just as a cup of cold water is more refreshing when you are parched. The first time you are filled, you may be so overwhelmed with His presence that you mark it down as a one-time event. Such powerful experiences have given rise to some unbiblical theologies and practices. But, according to the Bible, your Father wants to *repeatedly* fill you to the brim.

Because God must act upon you, in surrender you must let Him come on His own timetable. Only God knows when your heart is ready for the fullness of His Spirit. You cannot force God's hand. You cannot squeeze Him into a time frame. You can only wait. That is the command: "Wait until...."

Wait in Prayer

Not only must you wait, but you must wait in prayer. Prayer is opening your heart up to God, speaking to Him and listening to Him. Disciples in the New Testament frequently were filled with the Spirit while they were praying. Prayer is interacting with God and letting Him work in your heart.

God delights in your prayers. But we must explore which kinds of prayers God delights in. We must come to understand what types of prayers invite Him to clearly act in our lives.

Prayers God Delights In

Here are a few types of prayers that invite a demonstration of God's power in your life. These are not formulas but are examples from the Bible of the *postures* of heart that God delights in. The Bible makes it clear that God pours out His grace (His divine presence) when you humble your heart. Meditate on this overall posture:

> *Or do you suppose it is to no purpose that the Scripture says, "He yearns jealously over the spirit that he has made to dwell in us"? But he gives more grace. Therefore it says,* **"God opposes the proud but gives grace to the humble."** *Submit yourselves therefore to God. Resist the devil, and he will flee from you. Draw near to God, and he will draw near to you. Cleanse your hands, you sinners, and purify your hearts, you double-minded. Be wretched and mourn and weep. Let your laughter be turned to mourning and your joy to gloom. Humble yourselves before the Lord, and he will exalt you.* (James 4:5–10, emphasis added)

> *Clothe yourselves, all of you, with humility toward one another, for* **"God opposes the proud but gives grace to the humble."**

Humble yourselves, therefore, under the mighty hand of God so that at the proper time he may exalt you, casting all your anxieties on him, because he cares for you. (1 Pet. 5:5–7, emphasis added)

You are not just you waiting for God. He is waiting for you. He longs to draw near to you. He wants you to humble yourself before Him, and this frequently happens when you assume a prayerful posture.

> " YOU ARE NOT JUST YOU WAITING FOR GOD. HE IS WAITING FOR YOU. **HE LONGS TO DRAW NEAR TO YOU.** "

Picture it this way: your mind and your heart kneel before God and say "yes" to everything He identifies in your life. This is the ultimate illustration of humble prayer, which opens you to His divine presence.

Here are several postures of prayer that delight and are welcomed by God.

Prayer to Glorify God through Your Life

"Now is my soul troubled. And what shall I say? 'Father, save me from this hour'? But for this purpose I have come to this hour. **Father, glorify your name." Then a voice came from heaven: "I have glorified it, and I will glorify it again."** *The crowd that stood there and heard it said that it had thundered. Others said, "An angel has spoken to him." Jesus answered, "This voice has come for your sake, not mine. Now is the judgment of this world; now will the ruler of this world be*

cast out. And I, when I am lifted up from the earth, will draw
all people to myself." He said this to show by what kind of death
he was going to die. (John 12:27–33, emphasis added)

Jesus longed for His life to glorify the Father. In the four Gospels, we only know of three times that the Father audibly spoke from heaven to His Son: (1) at His baptism (a point of surrender), (2) on the mountain of transfiguration (another point of surrender), and (3) in this example just before His death. There was something so delightful to the Father in His Son's request that He thundered from heaven in response.

What posture of your heart calls God to thunder in response? What postures of your heart are so thrilling to the heart of God that He responds in clear ways that you can almost feel or hear? The most compelling prayer you can offer is that your life might bring the greatest honor, glory, and fame to the name of God.

Why? Because God wants you to make a name for Him, not for yourself. Surrender is about making God famous, not making you famous. Why wouldn't God show up when your only desire is to make Him famous in the entire world? This is the essence of the Great Commission in which Jesus promised His powerful presence to disciples who make His name known.

Too much of our modern Christianity is self-centered and abhorrent to God. We ask Jesus to "come into our hearts." God has no interest in coming into your heart when it is not surrendered. He does not want to come into *your* kingdom in power, but He wants you to come into *His* kingdom in surrender. You are not doing Him a favor by giving Him a *space* in your heart. He wants it *all*.

Too often we ask the wrong question: **"What is God's will for my life?"** That question is self-centered. It's about you and your life.

The right question is "What is God's will?" Period. And then, "How can my life best serve that?" To glorify God's name, you must understand what God is doing in our generation—what

> TOO OFTEN WE ASK THE WRONG QUESTION: **"WHAT IS GOD'S WILL FOR MY LIFE?"** THAT QUESTION IS SELF-CENTERED. IT'S ABOUT YOU AND YOUR LIFE. THE RIGHT QUESTION IS **"WHAT IS GOD'S WILL?"** PERIOD. AND THEN, **"HOW CAN MY LIFE BEST SERVE THAT?"**

He is about. Figure that out and then ask how you can best serve Him and His will.

◆ ◆ ◆

THE STORY LINE OF HISTORY: Following this chapter is a brief interlude in the S.W.A.P. explanation. It is critical at this point to understand what God has been doing throughout history and specifically in our generation. As you read that interlude, take time to wait in prayer and ask God what your part is in the story line of history.

◆ ◆ ◆

Practically, it takes planning and intentional action to surrender to God in this way. For example, a few years ago, my wife and I took several days at a lake house to wait on God and seek His direction for the next phase of our lives. We spent time separately, waiting on God in prayer, Bibles and journals open, pens in our hands. Periodically throughout the day we would get together to compare notes and discuss the implications of what God was saying. Then we would return to wait on God in prayer.

On the first day, we were not asking the right question. Rather than asking God, "What's next?" we needed to ask, "Father, what are You doing in our generation?" Only then could we figure out how to match our lives to His plans. Once we had allowed God to speak deeply to us about this, then we began to beg Him, "O Father, may we have some part in serving You in this purpose? We are just humble servants and want to do as You please. But if you would allow us to serve You, we will do it with all our hearts."

God showed up clearly that week. He showed us what He is up to in our generation and then gave us a clear mandate for the next phase of our lives.

Your Father is delighted when you pray in a similar way. Simply ask, "What is God's will, and how can my life most serve that?" Then you are on a path to making God famous in this world. Your prayer must be the same as Jesus's: "Father, glorify Your name! Make Yourself famous through me!"

God wants your whole being to bring glory to Him, not to yourself. The world is filled with individuals seeking their own glory, fame, and power. The kingdom of God must be populated with disciples seeking only *God's* glory, fame, and power. God will wait to show up in your life until this is the desire of your heart.

Here is an example of how to pray in this manner:

◆ ◆ ◆

PRAYER TO GLORIFY GOD

Father in heaven, you alone are the King. You alone deserve all the fame on this earth. I deserve none of it. I confess that my ambitions have too often been centered upon myself, my happiness, my control, my reputation, and my name. In my old nature, this was my natural way of living.

But I want to change all of that. It is hard because I don't know what You will say. But I know You are good and loving. Therefore, whatever You speak will be for Your great glory and my great delight. I only want to serve You and make You famous.

So, Father, I am asking You to show me how to make Your name more famous through my life. Glorify Your name through me! Forgive me for asking you, "What is Your will for my life?"

Instead, **show me Your will**. Period. Show me what You are doing in this world in our generation. Let my understanding be based on Your Word and not my own ideas. As You unfold Your will, then would you allow me the privilege of serving You and Your cause

in this world? Show me how my life can best serve You and make You most famous.

As Samuel prayed as child, so I pray, "Speak, for your servant hears" (1 Sam. 3:9). I surrender my dreams, aspirations, and hopes to live only for You. Make me someone who makes You famous!

◆ ◆ ◆

Prayer of Confession

God delights when we humble ourselves and confess our sin, inadequacies, and failings to Him. Why? Because it is an acknowledgement that He is God and we are not. We are the ones who go astray like sheep, not the Good Shepherd. The final verses in the longest chapter in the Bible end on this note:

Let my soul live and praise you,
and let your rules help me.
I have gone astray like a lost sheep; seek your servant,
for I do not forget your commandments. (Ps. 119:175–176)

The central purpose of Jesus's coming was to bring us back to God:

All we like sheep have gone astray;
we have turned—every one—to his own way;

and the Lord has laid on him
the iniquity of us all. (Isa. 53:6)

God loves to show up when you acknowledge your wandering heart and seek His forgiveness. A large part of the waiting process is letting God take the time to root out all sin and wandering in your life.

God promises to draw near to you when you draw near to Him in confession. As He cleanses you, He brings the sweetness of His presence into your life.

Draw near to God, and he will draw near to you. Cleanse your hands, you sinners, and purify your hearts, you double-minded. Be wretched and mourn and weep. Let your laughter be turned to mourning and your joy to gloom. Humble yourselves before the Lord, and he will exalt you. (James 4:8–10)

Though we will take a whole chapter to examine this aspect, here is an example of a prayer of confession. Remember, this is just an example of how to pray in an extended manner:

◆ ◆ ◆

PRAYER OF CONFESSION

O Father in heaven, You are righteous and I am not. Like a sheep, I have gone astray from You. My thoughts are not Your thoughts.

My own will has taken over in many areas of my life. And that is sin. I confess to You that I am sinful and need Your cleansing power in my life.

Shine Your light on my heart and show me every area in which I have gone astray from You. As David prayed, I pray as well:

Search me, O God, and know my heart!
Try me and know my thoughts!
And see if there be any grievous way in me,
and lead me in the way everlasting! (Ps. 139:23–24)

As You do, I will confess each sin to You and seek Your forgiveness. I want to be a clean vessel to honor You—a vessel in which Your Spirit can live and work.

Clean me thoroughly and make me whiter than snow. Let there be no impure thoughts, no unresolved relationship, and no offense that I have not made right.

I open my life before You right now. Cleanse me from all unrighteousness. Make me right before You.

◆ ◆ ◆

Prayer of Hunger for God

God knows that only He can bring you true joy and fulfillment. He wants you to want Him as your chief delight.

Only a life lived *in Him* can achieve its created design. He wants you to long for Him more than treasure. When you want Him more than any earthly thing, He is delighted and shows up in power. Psalm 42 is one example of this type of longing.

> *As a deer pants for flowing streams,*
> *so pants my soul for you, O God.*
> *My soul thirsts for God,*
> *for the living God.*
> *When shall I come and appear before God?* (Ps. 42:1–2)

Read the whole Psalm and meditate on it. The promise is that as you long for God and wait for Him, He will come in due time.

This longing for God was a large part of what the disciples prayed in the upper room in Acts 1. Their Master had left them. Jesus, who had spent three years visibly with them, was gone. As orphans, they prayed for His return. They longed for His presence. And the Spirit of Jesus honored the promise that had been given them:

> *"If you love me, you will keep my commandments. And I will ask the Father, and he will give you another Helper, to be with you forever, even the Spirit of truth, whom the world cannot receive, because it neither sees him nor knows him. You know him, for he dwells with you and will be in you. I will not leave you as orphans; I will come to you."* (John 14:15–18)

Too often we want…

>   …the *things* of God, but not *God*
>   …His *presents*, but not His *presence*
>   …the *fruit*, but not the *source*
>   …the *promises* of God, but not the *person* of God.

God wants to give you Himself, not just His promises. He is the treasure. He is the delight. Long for Him, and all the rest comes with Him. He is your portion, your inheritance:

> LORD, *you alone are my portion and my cup;*
> *you make my lot secure.*
> *The boundary lines have fallen for me in pleasant places;*
> *surely I have a delightful inheritance.* (Ps. 16:5–6, NIV)

> *Whom have I in heaven but you?*
> *And there is nothing on earth that I desire besides you.*
> *My flesh and my heart may fail,*
> *but God is the strength of my heart and my por-*
> *tion forever.* (Ps. 73:25–26)

When Moses was called up to the mountain to receive the Ten Commandments, he prayed the prayer of hunger for God and God passed by Him in all His glory:

Moses said, "Please show me your glory." And he [God] said, "I will make all my goodness pass before you and will proclaim before you my name 'The LORD.' And I will be gracious to whom I will be gracious, and will show mercy on whom I will show mercy. But," he said, "you cannot see my face, for man shall not see me and live." And the LORD said, "Behold, there is a place by me where you shall stand on the rock, and while my glory passes by I will put you in a cleft of the rock, and I will cover you with my hand until I have passed by. Then I will take away my hand, and you shall see my back, but my face shall not be seen." (Ex. 33:18–23)

The LORD passed before him and proclaimed, "The LORD, the LORD, a God merciful and gracious, slow to anger, and abounding in steadfast love and faithfulness, keeping steadfast love for thousands, forgiving iniquity and transgression and sin, but who will by no means clear the guilty, visiting the iniquity of the fathers on the children and the children's children, to the third and the fourth generation." And Moses quickly bowed his head toward the earth and worshiped. And he said, "If now I have found favor in your sight, O Lord, please let the Lord go in the midst of us, for it is a stiff-necked people, and pardon our iniquity and our sin, and take us for your inheritance." (Ex. 34:6–9)

God's heart was delighted by Moses's prayer to see God's glory and to welcome His presence. God's presence was so powerful that Moses's face shone when he came down from the mountain (Ex. 34:29). Moses received the presence of God, and with that, everything that comes with God.

Here is an example of how you can utter the prayer of hunger for God:

◆ ◆ ◆

PRAYER OF HUNGER

O Lord, You alone are my portion! You are the only inheritance I want. Wow! How delightful are the boundary lines of my inheritance in You! I delight in You and the portion You have given me in life.

O Father, show me Your glory. Show me more of You. For, I want You, not just Your promises. I want Your presence, not just your presents. I want Your Spirit, not just the fruit of Your Spirit.

You are my treasure and my reward. Let me not leave this place without Your clear and majestic presence in my life. I want to know You, the power of Jesus's resurrection, and the fellowship of His sufferings better (Phil. 3:10). Jesus, do not leave me like an orphan, but come to me. I long for Your presence.

Let me delight more in You, and my relationship with You, than in any earthly thing—any achievement, any relationship, any treasure, any aspiration, any interest, any hobby.

Like the man who found the treasure hidden in a field, I sell everything joyfully to have You (Matt. 13:44–45). Oh, give me Yourself! I am hungry. Let me taste and see that You are good! (Ps. 34:8).

Prayer of Surrender to God's Will

There are few passages in the Bible as moving as Jesus's prayer in the garden of Gethsemane. Jesus told his disciples that He was sorrowful even unto death (Mark 14:34). As He prayed to His father in the garden, He was in great agony about the next stages of the path. His sorrow was such that His sweat became like great drops of blood falling to the ground.

Put yourself in Jesus's sandals for a few minutes. Read this passage and meditate upon what it must have been like for the Son of God to choose to undergo torture, interrogation, and crucifixion. Think about what it must have been like for Him to be insulted and not insult in return—to be maligned, misunderstood, and accused of things He did not do. Think about what it was like for Him who had no sin to become sin on our behalf (2 Cor. 5:21). Meditate on this:

And he came out and went, as was his custom, to the Mount of Olives, and the disciples followed him. And when he came to the place, he said to them, "Pray that you may not enter into temptation." And he withdrew from them about a stone's

99

throw, and knelt down and prayed, saying, "Father, if you are willing, remove this cup from me. Nevertheless, not my will, but yours, be done." And there appeared to him an angel from heaven, strengthening him. And being in agony he prayed more earnestly; and his sweat became like great drops of blood falling down to the ground. And when he rose from prayer, he came to the disciples and found them sleeping for sorrow, and he said to them, "Why are you sleeping? Rise and pray that you may not enter into temptation." (Luke 22:39–46)

The agony of Gethsemane was so great that Jesus went back to His Father in prayer three times, each time asking for His Father's will to be done.

It is one thing to know what God's will is, but it is a different thing to surrender to it. That takes courage. Surrender to the will of God can be the most tortuous process of your life. For Jesus, it caused great agony, and it will for you as well. But that agony has great purpose. The beauty of surrender is born out of tears and travail. That is why you must wait on God in prayer. To submit to God and His ways is not easy, and you must take the time needed to get your heart in the right place. We all need Gethsemane experiences in our lives. They are the experiences that truly move the needle toward God's will being done.

> **"** WE ALL NEED **GETHSEMANE EXPERIENCES IN OUR LIVES.** **"**

The good news is that while Jesus was praying, angels came to minister to Him. This reminds us that God will intervene when you surrender to His will. He will give you the ability to find the courage to surrender.

The other good news is that when Jesus had finished praying, the spiritual courage and resolve He received enabled Him to finish what He started. Walking to the cross He never looked back. For the joy set before Him He endured its pain (Heb. 12:2).

The prayer of surrender is the prayer not only to *know* God's will but to have the courage to *do* it. Are you willing to pray for God to give you the courage to do whatever He leads you to do to glorify Him?

Take the time needed to get your heart to a place of surrender and courage. Take the time to get your heart to the point of delighting more in God's will than yours. It is not easy. It will cause great travail. If you will wrestle honestly with God about the implications of doing His will, and ask Him for the courage to do it, you will stay true to the terms of the contract He gives you. No looking back.

So often the will of God is clear. But what is not clear is our courage to walk it out. Pray for surrender. Pray for courage. Here is an example of how to do that:

PRAYER OF SURRENDER

O Father, I have prayed to know Your will. I have asked how my life can bring the greatest glory to You. I have prayed the

prayer of glorifying Your name. Now I understand better the implications of what that means. I have counted the cost. I know it will not be easy.

Father, I am scared to surrender. I lack the courage to obey. It is so much easier to do my will rather than Yours.

Yet, with my Lord Jesus, I pray, "Not my will, but Yours!" With clarity, remind me what Your will is and how I can best serve that. As You reveal that to me, give me the courage to say "yes" to You. I want to rise from this encounter with resolve to want Your will more than life itself.

I surrender my fears to You. I surrender my uncertainty. I know You will answer every question in due time. I know You will walk with me down this path, and that gives me great courage. I know that serving You will bring the greatest delight. With Jesus, I say, "My food is to do Your will and to accomplish Your work" (John 4:34).

Minister to me with Your angels. Minister to me with Your presence. This decision is not easy. Reassure my heart that surrender is good. Reassure my heart that You will uphold me.

Not my will, but Yours!

❖ ❖ ❖

Listening with Prayer and Fasting

Waiting in prayer must involve lots of listening to God. Prayer is a two-way conversation. Waiting on God in prayer should be filled with poring over the Word of God, journaling His words to you and your responses to Him, and praying in response to His promptings. Often God waits until your heart is in a position to receive Him in fullness. Can God trust the fullness of His Spirit to Your heart at this point in time?

The goal of your waiting time is to get your heart to a neutral place so that you would be delighted whether the answer is "yes" or "no," "this way" or "that way." You can achieve a neutral heart, open to anything God says or does, because this is the voice of your Beloved, and He knows what is best for your life and for His glory.

Hearing God and surrendering to Him during extended times of waiting often come most clearly in combination with fasting. In the Bible, God often shows up in power after His children not only pray but fast with purpose. Fasting is for the purpose of seeking God diligently, letting your hungry body remind you to pray. Fasting calls you to want God and His ways more than you want food.

Moses stayed upon the mountain of God for forty days, fasting the entire time, talking with God. When he returned to the bottom of the mountain, his face shone with the glory of God because He had been in conversation with God the whole time.

> *When Moses came down from Mount Sinai, with the two*
> *tablets of the testimony in his hand as he came down from*
> *the mountain, Moses did not know that the skin of his face*
> *shone because he had been talking with God.* (Ex. 34:29)

Jesus, full of the Spirit, was driven into the wilderness to be tempted for forty days. He fasted the entire time as He sought His Father at the beginning of His earthly ministry and resisted the temptations of the devil to take a different path. When He emerged from the wilderness fast, He described Himself as covered by the anointing of the Spirit:

> *And Jesus returned in the power of the Spirit to Galilee, and a re-*
> *port about him went out through all the surrounding country....*
> *He unrolled the scroll and found the place where it was written,*
>
> > *"The Spirit of the Lord is upon me,*
> > *because he has anointed me*
> > *to proclaim good news to the poor.*
> > *He has sent me to proclaim liberty to the captives*
> > *and recovering of sight to the blind,*
> > *to set at liberty those who are oppressed,*
> > *to proclaim the year of the Lord's favor." (Luke 4:18–19)*

Saul, who met Jesus in a divine experience on the road to Damascus, fasted and prayed for three days in the city of Damascus. What went through his mind as he recalled the horrors he had wreaked upon the people of God? What types of confession must have poured forth from his lips? Only after three days was he filled with the Spirit.

If you are earnestly seeking a breakthrough of the Spirit of God upon your life, consider adding to your prayerful waiting a period of fasting. It could be a complete fast from food. It could be a modified fast, depending on your health situation. Let God direct you on how to fast as you seek His face.[6]

Questions to Ponder

1. What are the biggest messages God has spoken to you while reading about the waiting in prayer process described in this chapter?
2. Review the "Prayers God Delights In" section. Which prayer do you most need to pray at this point in your life? Pray one of them right now.
3. The prayer of surrender is the prayer not only to know God's will but to have the courage to do it. Are you willing to pray for God to give you the

---

6 Medically speaking, it is dangerous to fast for more than forty days. Please consult your physician before embarking on a long period of fasting. Do not fast if you are pregnant or suspect you are pregnant. There are many good books which speak to this subject and discuss various types of fasting. Consider reading one in its entirety before walking this path.

courage to do whatever He shows you in the prayer to glorify Him?

4. Is there a need to take a period of time to fast for breakthrough? If so, schedule that now—preferably with a group of friends.

THE STORY LINE OF HISTORY

Too often, we ask the wrong question: **"What is God's will for my life?"** That question is self-centered. It's about you and your life.

The right question is, "What is God's will?" Period. And then, "How can my life best serve that?" To glorify God's name, you must understand what God is doing in our generation—what *He* is about.

To figure that out, you need to know what God is doing in history: the story line that began in Genesis 1 and will finish in Revelation 22. Then you can find your place in the historical plot.

God has a purpose for each generation to contribute to the plot:

> *David, after he had served the purpose of God **in his own generation**, fell asleep and was laid with his fathers.* (Acts 13:36, emphasis added)

David's life made a difference because he contributed to the plot of history as a protagonist—he was not just a side character in the story. He didn't stumble into this role accidentally. He became a protagonist because he had the right heart:

> *And when [God] had removed [King Saul], he raised up*
> *David to be their king, of whom he testified and said, 'I*
> *have found in David the son of Jesse **a man after my heart**,*
> *who will do all my will.'* (Acts 13:22, emphasis added)

In Abraham, the people of Israel were promised that they would (1) inherit the land and (2) become a blessing to all the nations of the Earth. The first step in that plan (taking the land) took one thousand years! It was not until God found a man after His own heart that Israel finally had rest from all of their enemies (2 Sam. 7:1). There was **no place left** for them to conquer.

Our Father's heart is the story line of history. He speeds up the pace of the plot when He finds protagonists who have *His* heart.[7]

> **OUR FATHER'S HEART IS THE STORY LINE OF HISTORY. HE SPEEDS UP THE PACE OF THE PLOT WHEN HE FINDS PROTAGONISTS WHO HAVE HIS HEART.**

---

7 It is not that God does not know when the final day will come. He is all-knowing and, of course, in perfect control. But from our perspective, when we see God moving in powerful ways through a surrendered person, the plot seems to speed up. Since we do not know the day and hour, we participate with God in the speeding up of the plot.

God often waits to fulfill His purposes until He finds such people who live for His purpose. But when he finds a person after his own heart, then the story line accelerates.

God is calling up a new generation that will not just be in the plot but that will *finish* the plot, hastening the story to its climax. A generation will one day say, "There is **no place left** for the kingdom of God to expand," as David did in the land of Canaan and the Apostle Paul did in the Eastern Roman Empire (Rom. 15:23).

Once you know the story line, you can take up your place in it, not as a side character but as a protagonist driven forward by the power of the Author. **Knowing the story line is knowing God's will.**

The grand story line began in Creation (Genesis 1) and ends at the Consummation (the return of Jesus; Revelation 22). It is the story of a great relay race to take the good news of the King to every lost place on earth. Each generation runs its own lap; each generation should accelerate the story line. But there will be a final generation that brings a climax to the story line because it runs the last lap—a generation that witnesses the King taking His reward for His history-long efforts.

There will be a last-lap generation. Why shouldn't it be us?

In our generation, God is doing something unprecedented in the story line. He is setting us up to finish the story—if we choose to accept the role.

Don't Forget the Story Line

In the last chapter of his life, Peter called followers of Jesus to remember their part in the story line. As his death drew near, he exhorted the church to keep the race of the kingdom going and not slacken the pace.

> *I think it right, as long as I am in this body, to stir you up by way of reminder, since I know that the putting off of my body will be soon, as our Lord Jesus Christ made clear to me. And I will make every effort so that after my departure you may be able at any time to recall these things.* (2 Pet. 1:13–15)

Peter had been living for the day of his Lord's return, playing his pivotal role in the story line. Before dying, he called disciples to speed up the story line, to hasten the climax—the day of God.

> *Since all these things are thus to be dissolved, what sort of people ought you to be in lives of holiness and godliness, waiting for and* **hastening the coming of the day of God**! (2 Pet. 3:11–12, emphasis added)

In the last chapter of his life, Peter stirred up sincere minds of Jesus-followers by way of reminder. Once more he reminded them of the grand purpose—the story line:

> *This is now the second letter that I am writing to you, beloved. In both of them* **I am stirring up your sincere mind by way**

of reminder, that you should remember the predictions of
*the holy prophets **and the commandment of the Lord and***
***Savior** through your apostles.* (2 Pet. 3:1–2, emphasis added)

Their hearts were sincere, but it was easy for them to forget the plot and lose their purposeful role. <u>Sincerity is no substitute for purposefulness</u> in the story line of history. Are you purposefully taking up your part in the story?

> 66 SINCERITY IS NO SUBSTITUTE FOR PURPOSEFULNESS IN THE STORY LINE OF HISTORY. 99

Peter reminded them of the story line given by the commandment of Jesus:

> *And this gospel of the kingdom will be proclaimed*
> *throughout the whole world as a testimony to all na-*
> *tions, and then the end will come.* (Matt. 24:14)

Do you know the story line? It's the grand race of Matthew 24:14 to bring the King's rightful reign to every tongue, tribe, people, and nation.

The Purpose of History

This fundamental story line runs throughout the Bible, weaving its way through each of the sixty-six books. Yet it is so easy to forget, and many scoff at such a thought:

> *Scoffers will come in the last days with scoffing, fol-*
> *lowing their own sinful desires. They will say, "Where*
> *is the promise of his coming? For ever since the*

> *fathers fell asleep, all things are continuing as they were*
> *from the beginning of creation."* (2 Pet. 3:3–4)

This reality describes our generation, not just Peter's. Individual Christians choose jobs based on personal achievement and monetary compensation rather than how their work can serve God's purposes. With no sense of plot to history, why spend our lives in service to the King? Rather, let's make money, have the possessions we want, raise a family in a comfortable environment, and live the dream. Eat, drink, and be merry.

The problem is that it is just a dream. The reality is that the coming of our Lord is a reality and He earnestly desires His children to make way for His coming by advancing the story line of history.

What is the story line of history?

- **CREATION:** In Genesis 1–2, **God created man-kind** for one purpose—to become a bride (companion) for His Son to dwell with Him forever in loving adoration.
- **FALL:** In Genesis 3, through sin, **mankind fell away** from God's design, no longer in relationship with the Creator.
- **SCATTERING:** In Genesis 11, languages were confused and **mankind was dispersed** to the ends of the earth, out of touch with the redemption of God.

- **PROMISE:** Starting in Genesis 12, **God promised to call the peoples of the Earth back** to Himself by the blood-price of a Redeemer through the good news–sharing efforts of the people of God (the descendants of Abraham).
- **REDEMPTION:** In the Gospels, **Jesus provided the price to pay the debt of sin to buy back** the people of God—people from every *ethne* (people group).
- **COMMISSION:** At the end of His earthly time, **Jesus launched the people of God to finish the mission** of God —the great story line—and promised His power to do so.
- **DISCIPLE-MAKING:** From the Book of Acts until today, the people of God have been blessed for one great mandate: **go into all the world and proclaim this redemption**, making disciples of every *ethne* to be the complete bride of Christ.
- **CONSUMMATION:** At the Consummation, **Jesus will return to take up His bride**—when she is complete and ready—from every tongue, tribe, people, and nation (Rev. 7:9).

Everything from Genesis 3 to Revelation 22 is about calling back Jesus's bride from among the nations. Until the bride is prepared, the mission of the church is not finished.

This is the story line Peter refers to in his last chapter.

> *But do not overlook this one fact, beloved, that with the Lord one day is as a thousand years, and a thousand years as one day. The Lord is not slow to fulfill his promise as some count slowness, but is patient toward you, not wishing that any should perish, but that all should reach repentance. But the day of the Lord will come like a thief, and then the heavens will pass away with a roar, and the heavenly bodies will be burned up and dissolved, and the earth and the works that are done on it will be exposed.* (2 Pet. 3:8–10)

God is patient. He will not send His Son back until the story line is finished. God is not slow, for he wants all *ethne* to come into His kingdom. Jesus tarries because His bride is not ready.

God does not wish any people group (*ethne*) to perish. He wants all of the dispersed nations of Genesis 11 to be a part of the bride of Christ in great number.

It is these *ethne* that Jesus referred to in Matthew 24:14. It is these *ethne* that He referred to in the Great Commission (Matt. 28:18–20: "make disciples of *ethne*"). It is these *ethne* that are pictured in Revelation:

> *After this I looked, and behold, a great multitude that no one could number, from every nation [ethne], from all tribes and peoples and languages, standing before the throne and before the Lamb.* (Rev. 7:9)

This is the climax of the story line of history: a ready bride presented to the Son with a great wedding banquet to celebrate. In Peter's last chapter, he refers to the gathering of this bride and also references Paul's writings:

> *Therefore, beloved, since you are waiting for these, be diligent to be found by him **without spot or blemish**, and at peace. And count the patience of our Lord as salvation, just as our beloved brother Paul also wrote to you according to the wisdom given him, as he does in all his letters.* (2 Pet. 3:14–16, emphasis added)

Paul refers to the same story line using the same words:

> *Christ loved the church and gave himself up for her, that he might sanctify her, having cleansed her by the washing of water with the word, so **that he might present the church to himself** in splendor, **without spot** or wrinkle or any such thing, that she might be holy and **without blemish**.... This mystery is profound, and I am saying that it refers to Christ and the church.* (Eph. 5:25–27, 32, emphasis added)

Paul refers to the same plan in Ephesians 1:

> *God has now revealed to us his mysterious will regarding Christ—which is to fulfill his own good plan. **And this is the plan: At the right time he will bring everything together under the authority of Christ—everything in heaven and on earth**. Furthermore, because we are united with Christ, we have received an inheritance from God, for he chose us*

> *in advance, and he makes everything work out according to his plan.* (Eph. 1:9–11, NLT, emphasis added)

God's plan from Creation to Consummation has been to regather people from every language and culture to return to the authority of Christ as His bride forever.

> GOD'S PLAN FROM CREATION TO CONSUMMATION HAS BEEN TO REGATHER PEOPLE FROM EVERY LANGUAGE AND CULTURE TO **RETURN TO THE AUTHORITY OF CHRIST AS HIS BRIDE FOREVER.**

But right now, that bride is incomplete. She is still missing an arm, an eye, and a foot. Her dress is still blemished and wrinkled. The bride is not yet ready. While the Bridegroom stands at the altar ready to wrap His bride in His arms, the bride seems to be in no hurry to get herself prepared for the wedding day.

But the posture of the bride is changing. This is one of the great distinctions of our generation, and it points us to the uniqueness of our chapter in the story line. Over the last two decades the global church has increased their pace to engage the more than eight thousand unreached people groups that remain in the world—the parts of the world still not represented by the bride in great numbers.

We have the end of the race in sight. We can see the edges of what remains—the places still left without clear gospel witness and the kingdom expanding.

But something even more exciting has developed in our chapter of history. Though this was a good first step, engagement of each people group was never the goal.

Reaching them completely was. And this is where things get thrilling.

The Spirit of God is accelerating the story line through His surrendered followers on every continent. And He is doing that through Acts-like movements—church-planting movements.

The only way to effectively reach the two billion people in the world who have no access to the gospel is through the kingdom of God exploding through them just as in the Book of Acts. Not reaching every one of them through outside missionaries, but by outside missionaries winning the first disciples who would then multiply their lives in the same way—generation by generation by generation.

Jesus told us to pray for the kingdom to come fully on Earth as in heaven (Matt. 6:9–10). This has always been our Father's heart—His kingdom coming powerfully and effectively in great torrents, not in mere trickles. He wants His kingdom to explode around you and in every dark place on earth.

In some dark days when our family worked in an unreached area of Asia, I came to a realization: unless the kingdom of God broke loose as in the book of Acts, we were sunk. There was no way we outside missionaries would be able to plant the five thousand churches needed to saturate our unreached people group. Even starting twenty churches a year would take us 250 years!

We needed a movement of disciples and churches multiplying by the power of the Spirit of God, not the power of foreign missionaries. For three and a half years we labored by God's power, but had little fruit—two disciples and no churches.

But when the Spirit of God broke loose, darkness turned to noonday. The first year, twenty-five new churches were started. The next year they multiplied to seventy-six. The following year they multiplied to 175. A church-planting or disciple-making movement had taken root in their discipleship.

When the gospel engages an unreached place, the kingdom of God must break loose. Jesus envisioned disciples making disciples making disciples. He desired churches planting churches planting churches. This is what happened in the Book of Acts. It was the DNA of early discipleship—that each disciple should be both a follower of Jesus and a fisher of men (Mark 1:17).

Jesus is not satisfied with a small or incomplete bride. He wants an uncountable number of people from each of the *ethne*. The only way to do so is through the kingdom multiplying in every one of them. Momentum is building for movements of God to become common again!

At the end of the 1990s, counting the movement we were a part of, I could count around eight to ten total church-planting movements (CPMs) in the world. In 2003, I estimated there were around thirty. In 2008, a group of colleagues and I estimated seventy-eight CPMs. As of October 2017, our coalition (called 24:14) has solid documentation of more than six hundred, with many other ministries close to the movement stage as well! That's 49 million new disciples and 3.6 million churches in twenty years.

Do you see what God is doing in our chapter of the story line? He is accelerating the timeline of history!

Although there are still thousands of unreached people groups and places that have no multiplying church among them, there is hope because of the Hidden Mover of movements. Though the gap is still great, the speed at which the gap is closing is quickening. God is hastening the day. The number of movements is rapidly multiplying.

The graph of movements is rising:

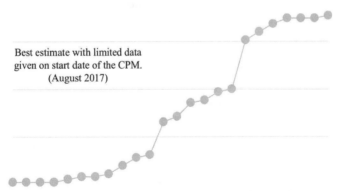

Increase in Church Planting Movements
Courtesy of the 24:14 Coalition

Best estimate with limited data given on start date of the CPM. (August 2017)

1995 1997 1999 2001 2003 2005 2007 2009 2011 2013 2015 2017

It's Acts time again.

Hasten the Day

After Peter reminded the early disciples of the plot, he called them to join God in speeding up the plotline toward its finale.

> *Since all these things are thus to be dissolved, what sort of people ought you to be in lives of holiness and godliness, **waiting for and hastening** the coming of the day of God!* (2 Pet. 3:11–12, emphasis added)

"Waiting for" means "to be in suspense," like when you cannot stop turning the pages of a thrilling book. Are you in suspense? Are you eagerly anticipating the finale of this grand plot? Are you anticipating the final lap of this great race of the kingdom?

God has given us an amazing privilege of joining Him in the race of history to accelerate the pace of the church toward the finish line. As you anticipate this day, you are called to hasten—or speed up—its arrival. We must rally God's people (the people of Abraham) around the world to become a mighty team, running with sacrifice toward the finale of the story line of history. The climax is in sight and by the power of the Spirit we can finish the story.

One of the greatest finishes—last laps—in swimming history came in the 2008 Beijing Olympics in the men's 4x100m freestyle relay. Michael Phelps and his three

American teammates were the underdogs. By the final lap, they were almost a full body length behind the leader. Three quarters through that last leg, unheralded Jason Lezak began to push harder than he ever had in his life. He sped up his pace beyond all expectations. In the last second he reached out to touch the wall to win. As the crowd went crazy, the announcer kept saying, "I can't believe it! It's not possible!" It was the most amazing final lap in modern Olympic history, and it was swum by someone relatively unknown.

Replays of that race reveal two groups hastening this extraordinary finish:

1. Lezak's three teammates standing at the finish line urging him to increase his pace
2. Lezak himself increasing his exertion beyond what appeared possible

A great cloud of witnesses—saints who have run their parts in the story before us (Heb. 12:1)—cheer us on, spurring us onward. What better way to honor their efforts than to finish what they contributed?

There will be a generation that speeds up its pace to finish what these others have begun. There will be a faith-filled, sacrificial effort by the power of the Spirit to exceed all expectations.

And then, when the Bridegroom is ready, He will return.

Make Haste to Play Your Role!

Before Peter signed off, he gave one last great call for the believers to make no delay in taking up their part:

> *So then, dear friends, since you are looking forward to this, make every effort [literally "make haste"] to be found spotless, blameless and at peace with him.* (2 Pet. 3:14, NIV)

Do you want to walk in the fullness of the Spirit? Do you long to see revival come to you, your church, or your organization? The answer is to make haste to *be* the type of people who are doing your part in the story line of history. When you serve the story line of history, the Father is thrilled to pour out His Spirit for that effort.

There is no shortage of the Spirit; just a shortage of willing recipients!

Surrendering to God's will means knowing His will for our generation. To what is He uniquely calling our generation? He is calling us to bring about the climax of history by the power of His Spirit.

How do you do that?

- **Make your life about reaching the unreached**, at home around you and to the ends of the earth. Pray, give, go (short term and long term), and advocate for them.
- **Reach them through kingdom movements** of multiplying disciples, groups, and churches. Contact us to learn how to see a movement start around you

and how to participate in similar movements around the world.

- **Do so with faith-filled, sacrificial urgency!** It is time for us to number our days that we may life wisely (Ps. 90:12). Make the sacrifices needed to finish the story.

A global coalition of movements—24:14—has arisen with this one overarching mandate: that every unreached people and place will be engaged with an effective kingdom movement strategy by 2025.[8] You need not take up your part in the story line alone.

God is calling us to take our generation to finish the story. Instead of writing a story that serves your own interests, jump into God's story. Become a protagonist in the story, not a side character. Contact us to learn how you can hasten the day.

> " BECOME A PROTAGONIST IN THE STORY, NOT A SIDE CHARACTER. "

All of us in this global coalition are a volunteer army. We do it for the love of our King no matter the jobs we have that pay the bills.

There will be a final generation that brings the climax to the story, in the day of God's power:

> *Your people will volunteer freely [literally "become freewill offerings"] in the day of Your power;*

---

8 See 2414now.net for how you can get involved, no matter your profession.

In holy array, from the womb of the dawn, Your
youth are to You as the dew. (Ps. 110:3, NASB)

They will do it because, in their love for the Bridegroom, they long to bring in His bride. They will become freewill offerings (volunteers) for that effort. They will become so numerous that they will cover the Earth like dew and will be a holy people in the midst of a wicked and perverse generation.

Can we be the final generation?

Will you join this generation?

The question is: "What is God's will?" Period.

Then ask, "How can my life best serve that purpose in this generation?"

Jesus promises His powerful presence to all who join in that effort (Matt. 28:20).

Someone will finish the story. Why not us?

Questions to Ponder

1. Can you state in your own words the story line of history?
2. How does this make sense of what is going on around us?
3. Where does your life fall between being a side character and a protagonist?

4. How could your life best hasten the plot of history so that you become a protagonist, not a side character?

CHAPTER 6

S.W.A.P. – WAIT ON GOD IN PRAYER (PART 2)

Since being filled is a passive idea—that God must act upon us—we must wait on Him in prayer, just as Jesus commanded the disciples to do in the days leading up to Pentecost. As was noted earlier, God longs to draw near to you. He is waiting for you; you're not just waiting for Him. He wants you to humble yourself before Him, and this frequently happens in a prayerful posture.

> **S**urrender to His will and His every word
> **Wait on God in prayer**
> **A**void sin and let God root out all unrighteousness
> **P**ursue the promptings of the Spirit

In the Bible, waiting on God in prayer takes two forms: longer periods and shorter periods of waiting. Let's call the former "forty-day times" and the latter "frequent forays." During those times, disciples prayed the various types of prayers mentioned in the previous chapter.

Forty-Day Times–The Deep Work

In the Bible, examples of disciples being filled with the Spirit of God for the first, second, or third time frequently involved longer periods of waiting. For example:

- Moses fasting on Mt. Sinai for forty days (Ex. 34:28)
- Jesus fasting in the wilderness for forty days (Matt. 4:2)
- The disciples praying in the upper room for ten days (Acts 1:13–14)
- Saul of Tarsus in prayer fasting in Damascus for three days (Acts 9:9–11)

Let's figuratively call these "forty-day times" based on the examples of Moses and Jesus. During these periods of time, God worked in remarkable ways with His servants.

If you are serious about being full of the Spirit, then you must also be serious about taking the time to wait on God for that to happen. Today's fast-paced culture is entirely unsuited to the filling of the Spirit. Today's "three-simple-steps-to" society is entirely unsuited to waiting for God to act. Today's can-do mindset is entirely unsuited to the active passivity of tarrying until God comes in power.

> TODAY'S "THREE-SIMPLE-STEPS-TO" SOCIETY IS **ENTIRELY UNSUITED TO WAITING FOR GOD TO ACT.**

There is no shortcut to the fullness of the Spirit. It takes time. God will show up in power when He decides, not when you dictate.

In the upper room, the disciples were completely focused on God and His purposes. Away from their own homes, they bound themselves together to wait upon God. The way that disciples in the Bible fostered encounters with God was through lengthy periods of waiting where they were not disturbed.

The first time Moses encountered God in power, it happened in the most distant and desolate locale of his life.

> *Now Moses was tending the flock of Jethro his father-in-law, the priest of Midian, and he led the flock to **the far side of the wilderness** and came to Horeb, the mountain of God. There the angel of the LORD appeared to him in flames of fire from within a bush.* (Ex. 3:1–2, NIV, emphasis added)

The Bible does not spell out the length of this encounter with God at the burning bush. Very likely, it was not simply a one-hour conversation. This was not Moses's "daily quiet time." It was longer and much more dramatic than what can be accomplished in a few minutes alone with God.

At the far side of the wilderness, Moses was removed from any distractions. He was alone with God and the sheep. God worked in Moses's life in two remarkable ways. First, He gave Moses a mission; second, He responded to every objection.

Moses had time to work through each objection with persistence and God had time to answer each through His loving patience. Such encounters with God are only fostered in an *unhurried time*. As Moses arrived at a place of surrender, God promised His special presence to go with Moses. Moses had enough time to work through his objections one by one.

Similarly, the prophet Elijah fasted and prayed during a time of great turmoil for forty days (1 Kings 19:8). In the wilderness, on the mountain of God, Elijah shared with the Lord his difficulties, his zeal for God's honor and his deep concerns. In this lengthy period, Elijah plumbed the depths of depression and despair. God answered Elijah in a gently tangible way, not in the mighty rushing wind, the earthquake, or the fire, but in the stillness of a whisper. Elijah had time to work through his concerns in God's presence.

Likewise, during Jesus's forty days in the wilderness, the enemy tempted our Lord to divert Him from His mission as the Suffering Servant. He offered the Messiah a false path toward the same goal. The forty days gave time for Jesus to be tested and to declare to the enemy what type of Messiah He would be.

And then Saul, the persecutor of the church, fasted and prayed for three days in the city of Damascus. In all likelihood, God was giving him time to evaluate the repercussions of his previous life. Paul referred back to his sin of persecuting the church for the remainder of his life.

> *For I am the least of the apostles, unworthy to be called an apostle, because I persecuted the church of God. But*

> *by the grace of God I am what I am, and his grace toward me was not in vain. On the contrary, I worked harder than any of them, though it was not I, but the grace of God that is with me.* (1 Cor. 15:9–10)

God allowed His servant to move to a place of humility and surrender. He allowed His servant a chance to count the cost of the mission God was giving him. God told Ananias, who prayed for Paul,

> *"Go, for he is a chosen instrument of mine to carry my name before the Gentiles and kings and the children of Israel. For I will show him how much he must suffer for the sake of my name."* (Acts 9:15–16)

Saul had time to work through the implications of this radical turn in his life: to confess the old, receive forgiveness, and count the cost of the mission.

The only way to foster lengthy periods of waiting is to get alone in a place where you will not be disturbed. An ideal situation is to take several days away at a retreat venue, a cabin in the woods, a vacation home, even a tent at a campsite. Find a place where you can change your environment, leave the demands of life and work behind, and focus entirely on God. Put away email, work texts, web browsing, and social media. Go on a fast from these to seek your Father.

Your goal is to get your heart to a place in which He can entrust Himself more fully to you. After Simon the magician professed faith in Jesus, he saw the subsequent power of the Spirit in the life of Peter and John. His heart, however, was wrong. He longed for the *power*, not the *person* of God:

> *Now when Simon saw that the Spirit was given through the laying on of the apostles' hands, he offered them money, saying, "Give me this power also, so that anyone on whom I lay my hands may receive the Holy Spirit." But Peter said to him, "May your silver perish with you, because you thought you could obtain the gift of God with money! You have neither part nor lot in this matter, **for your heart is not right before God.**"* (Acts 8:18–21, emphasis added)

Having the right heart is the foundation for the Spirit of God to show up in power in your life. If you were about to have heart surgery using one of the most advanced surgical machines of our generation, would you entrust yourself to a first-year medical student who had not yet mastered that device? You would only trust a licensed cardiac surgeon who had spent many hours of practice and implementation to use such a powerful machine on such a sensitive place of your body. Such power should only be used by people who have had the training, discipline, steadfastness, and level-headedness to use it properly.

Why would God give the power of His Spirit to a heart He cannot trust?

Are you the kind of person God would use?

Are you the kind of person to whom God would entrust the power of His Spirit?

Are you the kind of person to whom God would entrust a movement of His kingdom?

> ARE YOU THE KIND OF PERSON TO WHOM **GOD WOULD ENTRUST THE POWER OF HIS SPIRIT?**

God's entrusting of His Spirit to you is not based on the height of your spiritual attainment, rather the posture of your heart. He's not looking for spiritual giants; only surrendered hearts. Right now, you have the option to humble yourself and become that person.

A "forty-day" time with God should involve allowing a sufficient period for God to show up. Take some vacation days and get away with God. A guide is included at the end of this book that breaks down how to do this. It is a guide that helps you meet with God. I call it a "SWAPmeet," which is an extended time for you to meet with God and S.W.A.P. your control for His. Also included in the back is a guide for your small group, church, or organization to wait on God for several evenings or days, surrendering yourselves afresh and asking Him to show up as in days of old.

The Sweet Honeymoon

It is here that the analogy of marriage especially helps us. After a couple takes their vows of surrender on their wedding day, they normally follow with a period to get away with each other—a honeymoon. Regardless of the length of time it spans, a honeymoon is meant to draw spouses closer together. It's easy to tell when a pair of newlyweds have just returned from their honeymoon. Their eyes sparkle. They cannot turn loose of each other. They cannot stop talking about each other. They are in love.

Many years ago, my wife and I learned a discipline for our marriage that fosters intimacy. Every five years we take another lengthy honeymoon to rekindle the flames of our marriage. In between those honeymoons, if we see that our intimacy and tenderness is lagging, we get away for a night or two for a mini-honeymoon.

Whether long or short, our agenda during these honeymoons is just to focus on each other. No email, no work, no phone calls. We are simply alone together. When we return from these honeymoons, you can see it in us. Our eyes sparkle. We cannot turn loose of each other. We want to talk about each other with anyone we meet. These honeymoons continue to rekindle the flames of our relationship after three decades of marriage.

On our honeymoons, my wife and I do not seek *intimacy*. Instead, we seek *each other*. I focus on my wife, her needs, her amazing qualities, and why I married her in the first place. I serve her, pamper her, and bless her. I lavish myself upon her. I demonstrate exceptional tenderness to her. She does the same with me. We put each other first and make one another feel special. We become freshly enamored with each other.

During these times, not only do we show each other tenderness and affection, but we talk about deeper issues of life. It takes time to work through these issues and figure out how we should respond to them. Only prolonged periods of time give us the margin to go deep in conversation. We discuss our priorities, our hopes, and our plans.

We find that the demands of normal life are such that we cannot usually talk in depth about these topics on a daily basis. But honeymoons allow us enough time to go deep and wrestle through issues in a loving, intimate relationship. They serve as markers to keep us on the right track and in right relationship. They are the pillars around which we build daily times of talking and weekly dates that maintain intimacy and help us make course corrections.

Forty-day times, or SWAPmeets, with your Father can best be viewed as honeymoons with your Beloved. Whether it's for two nights or for two weeks, the goal is to return to the intimacy of your love relationship with God. Yes, you want to be filled afresh with the Spirit. But your goal is not an experience. Your goal is intimacy with God. Period. Beware of seeking an experience instead of seeking the God of that experience. Beware of seeking the effect of the Spirit rather than the Spirit Himself.

Your goal is also to hear from Him so that He can set priorities for the next stage of your life. He wants to show you His plans for the steps ahead. He wants to root out sin. He wants to talk to you about deeper things than He can when you only give him fifteen, thirty, or sixty minutes a day in your quiet time. Your goal is to listen to Him and become more in awe of Him. Your goal is to fall freshly in love with your Maker.

When you plan your SWAPmeet, aim for the maximum time you can take rather than the minimum. Plan time for God to go deep with you. My wife and I would love for most of our honeymoons to be longer. Wouldn't you love to have longer, uninterrupted time with your Beloved?

If disciples of Jesus today would simply take these longer periods of time away with God solely to focus on Him, the church at large would be revived. If disciples of Jesus would spend long times alone with Him, His priorities would become theirs.

Frequent Forays–Staying Filled

But now even more the report about him went abroad, and great crowds gathered to hear him and to be healed of their infirmities. But he would withdraw to desolate places and pray. (Luke 5:15–16)

Jesus experienced dramatic encounters with the Spirit of God filling Him. At His baptism, a point of absolute surrender to the ministry His Father was giving Him, Jesus was filled with the Holy Spirit. The Father spoke audibly from heaven,

> *"You are my beloved Son; with you I am*
> *well pleased"* (Luke 3:22).

The wilderness time was another dramatic encounter with the Father, led by the Spirit (Luke 4:1). His return from the wilderness was marked with the fullness of the Spirit (Luke 4:18).

Those lengthy, dramatic encounters with the Spirit of God were important in His life. Even so, Jesus frequently made forays into the wilderness to be alone with His Father. As Jesus's popularity grew, and the demands from the crowds became stronger, He maintained the priority of withdrawing to lonely places where He could pray. They were frequent forays—excursions—to meet with His Father.

What happened during these forays? The Scripture hints at the answer by mentioning them during times of increased demand upon the life of Jesus.

For instance, in Mark 1, Jesus experienced a full day of fruitful ministry in the town of Capernaum—the whole town was affected by His preaching and healing. Jesus fell asleep late in the evening. What did he do the next morning?

> *And rising very early in the morning, while it was*
> *still dark, he departed and went out to a deso-*
> *late place, and there he prayed.* (Mark 1:35)

Jesus made one of His frequent forays to meet with His Father. What was the object of His prayer? I believe Jesus was asking His Father for perspective on what to do with the previous day's success. He was listening to the Father and reaffirming His commitment to the path to which He had surrendered. Jesus modeled absolute reliance on the Father's leading. He gives a glimpse of this lifestyle in another passage:

> *So Jesus said to them, "Truly, truly, I say to you, the Son can do nothing of his own accord, but only what he sees the Father doing. For whatever the Father does, that the Son does likewise. For the Father loves the Son and shows him all that he himself is doing." (John 5:19–20)*

In Mark 1, while Jesus was praying, the disciples searched for Him and finally found Him. They told Him what almost anyone in ministry would like to hear: "Everyone is looking for You."

Jesus, however, defied their expectations. Rather than stay and build on this success, He chose to move on.

> *And he said to them, "Let us go on to the next towns, that I may preach there also, for that is why I came out." And he went throughout all Galilee, preaching in their synagogues and casting out demons. (Mark 1:38–39)*

The success of the previous day could have enticed anyone to stay and linger. Instead, Jesus stayed on the mission to go throughout all Galilee. He stuck to the script the Father gave Him. Jesus's frequent forays to meet with His Father kept His life centered on the Father and His glory.

Similarly, Luke 5:15 gives us context for Luke 5:16 (the frequent forays):

> *But now even more the report about him went abroad, and great crowds gathered to hear him and to be healed of their infirmities. But he would withdraw to desolate places and pray.* (Luke 5:15–16)

As Jesus's fame spread, His times with the Father were highlighted in the Scripture text. Jesus filtered every experience and every day through times away with His Father in prayer. So must we.

It is one thing to fill the wineskin of your life with the new wine of the Spirit. But it is another thing to keep it topped up and full at every moment. There are times when the wineskin becomes completely empty; it needs the refilling of forty-day times. But for most days, we simply need to keep it topped up. These top-up times come when we pull away frequently to linger with our Father.

Every disciple needs both types of encounters with God. You need the longer periods of time for Him to do a deeper work in your heart. But you also need to develop the discipline of staying in His presence. You need the discipline of staying full of His Spirit. Staying full comes with frequent forays into the prayer closet or your quiet time chair. Your frequent forays with God can include a hike in the woods or a time of prayer near a lake—any place you feel safe and comfortable to meet God. These times help you stay surrendered day by day.

The Goal of Your Quiet Time

Each day, preferably in the morning, you need *unhurried* time alone with God to *linger* in His presence. We often call this "quiet time" or "devotional time." The goal of this time is not to check it off your daily list of spiritual disciplines every growing believer should engage in. The goal is not to ensure that God blesses your day by starting the day with Him.

The goal of your quiet time is to make sure that you are *still* surrendered. The goal of this time is to meet with God, hear Him, and surrender to His plans for that day. Your quiet time is a chance once more to sign the blank page of surrender to every word of Christ.

A quiet time is not the same thing as abiding in Christ. The aim of quiet time is to launch you into walking in the Spirit or abiding in Christ *throughout* the day. That morning time is your date with God, which allows you to stay connected to Him all day long. Abiding in Christ is a through-the-day posture of your heart.

> " A QUIET TIME IS NOT THE SAME THING AS ABIDING IN CHRIST. **THE AIM OF QUIET TIME IS TO LAUNCH YOU INTO WALKING IN THE SPIRIT** OR ABIDING IN CHRIST THROUGHOUT THE DAY. "

George Mueller (1805–1898) was a well-known servant of Jesus. During his life in England, he supported several orphanages financially, and he did so completely through prayer. He resolved that all the money he needed would come through petitioning His Father in heaven to move men's hearts. Thus, He never asked any human for money. Not one day went by that Mueller did not receive the provision needed for hungry children.

Part of the key to his faith was the way Mueller started each day. His perspective was that his daily time with the Lord had one goal: **to have his soul become happy in the Lord.**

I saw more clearly than ever, that the first great and primary business to which I ought to attend every day was, **to have my soul happy in the Lord**. The first thing to be concerned about was not, how much I might serve the Lord, how I might glorify the Lord; but how I might get my soul into a happy state, and how my inner man may be nourished…I saw that the most important thing I had to do was to give myself to the reading of the Word of God and to meditation on it.

According to my judgment the most important point to be attended to is this: above all things see to it that your souls are happy in the Lord. Other things may press upon you, the Lord's work may even have urgent claims upon your attention, but I deliberately repeat, it is of supreme and paramount importance that you should seek above all things to have your souls truly happy in God Himself! Day by day seek to make this the most important business of your life. This has been my firm and settled condition for the last five and thirty years. For the first four years after my conversion I knew not its vast importance, but now after much experience I specially commend this point to the notice of my younger brethren and sisters in Christ: **the secret of all true effectual service is joy in God, having experimental acquaintance and fellowship with God Himself**.[9]

Let Mueller be an example to you. His faith emerged from his times alone with his Father, making his soul happy in the Lord. Part of becoming happy in the Lord was his ability to get his heart to a place of neutrality, or surrender.

Your time alone with the Father each morning should be for this purpose. That is why you need unhurried time with God. Linger with God until your soul is happy.

How can you make your daily quiet time a reality? I suggest you designate a location for your quiet time. Mine is a big, comfy, leather armchair that swallows me

9 *A Narrative of Some of the Lord's Dealing with George Muller, Written by Himself, Jehovah Magnified. Addresses by George Muller Complete and Unabridged*, 2 vols. (Muskegon, Mich.: Dust and Ashes Publications, 2003) 2:730–31. http://www.desiringgod.org/messages/george-muellers-strategy-for-showing-god#67. (Author's emphasis added.)

up. On the back I have a throw blanket to wrap up in on cool mornings. Next to my chair is a shelf where I keep my Bible, journal, pens, and Bible helps. Above that is where I put my coffee thermos and my cup.

To facilitate me designating this as a date with God, I change the lighting in the room, which normally is my office. I have a special lamp next to my leather chair that shines onto my Bible and reminds me to seek God. I keep my laptop a long way from that chair so that I am not tempted to get drawn into the day's busyness or distracted by the enticing screen.

I'll let you in on another secret: when the weather is good, I sneak outside to an alternate spot where I can hear the birds awaken with the dawn. Sometimes the change of environment reminds me that the goal is to seek God, not to mark off my "daily quiet time" from my spiritual to-do list.

Having a designated place (and perhaps an alternate place) and time for your quiet time helps it become a regular discipline of your life so that you can experience God.

What if you have small kids who need tending? This is a great opportunity for you and your spouse to figure out how to tag-team taking care of the kids so each of you can have time alone with God. If you are a single parent, you may need to set the alarm to help you beat the kids awake. Alternatively, you might be able to get a college student to drop by on several mornings for thirty to sixty minutes to give them some "kid" time and free you up for this important daily date. Then you could invite that student to stay a bit longer to hang out for breakfast—even just a bowl of cereal.

You can apply these simple principles to any frequent foray with God, even those beyond your quiet time place. You can follow these applications on a hike in the woods, a stroll by a lake, or nestled by an outdoor fire pit.

Dates with God

Early on in my Christian life God gave me the image that my quiet time was my date with God. I love dates with my wife. I anticipate them. I rush to them. I cannot wait for that time for us to savor each other alone. Especially when the kids were small, we could not wait for the babysitter to arrive so we could escape to each other.

Quiet time is no different. It's an escape to meet with your Father in secret, to foster intimacy with Him, just as He wishes.

> *When you pray, go into your room and shut the door and pray to your Father who is in secret. And your Father who sees in secret will reward you.* (Matt. 6:6)

But it's not just that. God desires the time to *linger*. On a date with my wife, looking at my watch frequently does not foster intimacy. My wife wants me for unhindered, focused time with her. She wants me to pay more attention to her than the time. Early in parenthood, getting such unhurried time was difficult but worth it. And now that we are empty nesters, we still find that we need to break up the weekly routine by having dates that foster intimacy.

Your Beloved is calling you to unhurried times to linger in His presence and meet with Him.

In addition to date nights, my wife and I have also learned the discipline of a daily "wake-up" time together. When our three sons were very small, we never seemed to find any sane moments to be alone together to connect as a couple. From the break of dawn until we plopped ourselves in bed exhausted, our attention was on our kids' desires and needs. In the evening, no matter our good intentions, we were too exhausted to connect deeply.

One week, the pattern of our marriage changed. We resolved to wake before our kids so we could have time alone together. I bought a coffee maker with a built-in timer and placed it on the dresser in our bedroom. At the end of the day, I scooped the coffee grounds into the filter basket, filled up the reservoir with water, and set the timer for 5:15 a.m.

The first few mornings were very difficult. At 5:15, as the coffee started brewing, slowly our eyelids would begin fluttering. I would stagger across the room and pour two cups of coffee. Carefully I would make my way back to the bed where we propped ourselves up and began sipping. At first, very little meaningful conversation took place, but we had woken before the boys! That alone was success. But as the caffeine began to course through our veins, we became civilized human beings, and soon the conversation flowed.

Over time, this became an important part of our daily routine. During these moments, we would connect our hearts, talk about life, and often pray together. Starting the day that way enabled us to stay connected and intimate throughout the day. The goal of our time was to get our hearts happy with each other before the craziness of the day took hold.

In the beginning, so as not to set ourselves up for failure, we only attempted these early morning wake-ups four days a week. This way, we had permission to sleep longer three other mornings. Slowly, however, this practice transformed our relationship as a married couple with kids at home. Over the last three decades, scarcely a morning has gone by that I have not brought coffee to my wife in bed. Each day we prop ourselves up, cradle the cups in our hands, and talk about life. Even with an empty nest, it feels great to get our hearts connected and happy with each other before the craziness of the day takes hold.

For my wife and me, daily wake-up times and weekly dates are frequent forays into an intimate place to connect our hearts together. Add to that our periodic honeymoons, and you can see the cadence that built intimacy and unity in our marriage.

Relationship with God is no different. You need both forty-day times and frequent forays to build a cadence of intimacy with God that fosters walking in the Spirit.

You need frequent intimate forays alone with God in which you spend enough time to linger over His Word and let Him speak to you afresh. Some of those will be shorter (think coffee wake-ups) and some will be longer (think weekly date nights).

You cannot walk in the Spirit only through the occasional stronger experiences that come with forty-day times. You must also stay topped up in the fullness of the Spirit, and that only comes through getting away daily with your Father in secret. In those moments, He will continue making course corrections to the surrender of your life. He will continue to write terms on the blank sheet of your life. He will give you an opportunity to stay surrendered. He will reconnect with you.

The longer you stay surrendered, the longer you walk in the fullness of the Spirit. You stay surrendered through staying fresh with God.

There will come a time when you begin to pull back from your surrender and will need to get away for a longer period of intimacy with your Father. You will need a fresh filling of the Spirit. That's when you'll need to plan forty-day time (SWAPmeet). However, daily times alone with Him will lengthen the time that you can stay walking in the Spirit of God.

Active Waiting

Waiting on God in prayer can sound like a passive event and, in many ways, it is. God must *act* upon you. But waiting in prayer is also an intensely *active* time—it's not just you waiting for God to act upon you, but actively searching for Him, delighting yourself in Him, surrendering every part of your heart, confessing every sin, seeking to bring Him the greatest glory, and counting every cost of the path ahead.

You must actively wait for God to act upon you. Throughout the "waiting" period—whether long or short—God is actively interacting with you, calling you to respond to Him. You respond and then He speaks again, calling you to respond. This two-way interaction—reading your Bible, recording what God is saying in your journal, praying your responses to Him, asking Him questions, listening—is an active waiting.

Waiting on God in prayer is not emptying yourself and waiting for enlightenment. That is an Eastern concept of meditation. Rather, it is an active seeking of God, filling yourself up with His Word, and going deep with Him. Look at the example of Moses on the mountain before God and the amazing conversations they had over forty days. Moses actively waited on the Creator.

Scheduling a SWAPmeet

One outcome of reading this book should be that you schedule time to get away with God for several days by planning a SWAPmeet. The point is to actively wait on God through the S.W.A.P. process over a weekend or several days. If married, you may need to let your spouse do the same thing by choosing to take care of the kids for a weekend to let him or her get away. Perhaps as a single person you would want to give this as a gift to a couple with young kids so that they can take time for a SWAPmeet.

I would also encourage you to schedule a SWAPmeet, perhaps as a weekend retreat, with a group of friends. During a SWAPmeet, it is easy for your mind to wander and priorities to slip when you are alone. It takes discipline to stay focused on God. But if you have friends who share the same goal, they can help you stay diligent about meeting God. During the SWAPmeet, you can meet up periodically to discuss what God is saying to you and to encourage one another. Look at the resources at the back of this book for suggestions on how to do this. Right now is a good time to put a SWAPmeet on the calendar. Before you read any further, block some time off and let nothing violate that timeframe. Physically marking the time as busy makes it easier to make the time a priority. If anyone wants to make an appointment with you during that time, you can say, "I already have a commitment." And it couldn't be more true. Because you've got a commitment to spend time with your Beloved being filled afresh.

Questions to Ponder

1. Are you the kind of person to whom God would entrust the power of His Spirit? God's entrusting of

His Spirit is not based on the height of your spiritual attainment, rather the posture of your heart. What needs to change within you to refine that posture?

2. How does viewing a longer getaway with God as a "honeymoon" help you in thinking about how to meet with Him?

3. How does viewing daily quiet times as a "date" with God help you in thinking about how to meet with Him? Can you identify with George Mueller that the goal of your quiet time is to get your soul happy in Jesus?

4. Now that you have scheduled your SWAPmeet, how do you envision it unfolding? Will you do it by yourself or with friends?

5. If with a group, discuss with your group when and where your daily quiet time will unfold. How can you set up to designate it as a date with God? If alone, how can you build a schedule and hold yourself accountable?

CHAPTER 7

S.W.**A**.P. – __A__VOID SIN AND LET GOD ROOT OUT ALL UNRIGHTEOUSNESS

The first three aspects of the S.W.A.P. framework are *simultaneous* not *sequential*. They are three parts of the same process that lead to the final piece of the framework—being led by the Spirit in power.

In the previous two chapters we examined the second element of the biblical framework—__w__ait on God in prayer. The surrendering process (Chapter 4) and the confessing process described in this chapter are best achieved through actively waiting on God in prayer (Chapters 5 and 6). As discussed, we need our daily "dates" with God to keep us surrendering, confessing, and following His leading. Sometimes, though, we need longer times to get away to let Him do a deep work.

One of the reasons we often need extended time away is that the Convictor, Forgiver, and Restorer wants an unhurried process of rooting out sin in our lives. But the Sustainer wants to move us past the point of confession into restoration of a harmonious relationship. He wants to maintain us in a place of holiness in which we **avoid sin in our lives.** This is the third pillar of the S.W.A.P. process.

Surrender to His will and His every word
Wait on God in prayer
Avoid sin and let God root out all unrighteousness
Pursue the promptings of the Spirit

The third Person of the Trinity is the **Holy** Spirit. He fills and guides a **holy** vessel, not an unholy one. If we are going to embark upon the Spirit Walk—being led by the Spirit—we must abandon the indulgence of sin and instead indulge in the abandonment of right living. The Father is offering you a choice to be led by the Spirit or not.

> *For those who live according to the flesh set their minds on the things of the flesh, but those who live according to the Spirit set their minds on the things of the Spirit. For to set the mind on the flesh is death, but to set the mind on the Spirit is life and peace. For the mind that is set on the flesh is hostile to God, for it does not submit to God's law; indeed, it cannot. Those who are in the flesh cannot please God.* (Rom. 8:5–8)

The Holy Spirit Is a Person Who Can Be Grieved or Offended

It is easy to think of the Holy Spirit as an impersonal force in your life. With an impersonal force, the stakes are much lower. This is the *Star Wars* perspective: personal holiness has nothing to do with the ability to channel *the Force*. If the Holy Spirit were an impersonal force, then you could live however you like.

But the Holy Spirit is a *person*. He is the Spirit of Jesus who has come to dwell in your life. Since He is a person, He can be offended, or grieved, like any other person. You must understand the nature of the person you have invited to come into your life to reside as a guest. Just as you consider how to make human guests in your home welcome, so you must understand the nature of the Spirit. Your goal must be that He would be perfectly at ease in every room of your life.

The most commonly quoted verse on being filled with the Spirit is found in Ephesians:

> *And do not get drunk with wine, for that is debauchery, but be filled with the Spirit.* (Eph. 5:18)

However, to understand this verse correctly, we must put it in context near the end of a lengthy passage starting in Ephesians 4:17 an ending in Ephesians 5:21. The headings in many Bibles for this section may be things like "The Christian's Walk," "Imitators of God," "The New Life," "Instructions for Christian Living," and so on.

This passage sets up and finds its culmination in Ephesians 5:18. In these thirty-six verses, Paul emphasizes that ***the filling of the Spirit is an outcome of rooting out sin***. We must make our

> **WE MUST MAKE OUR HEARTS A COMFORTABLE PLACE FOR THE HOLY SPIRIT OF GOD.**

hearts a comfortable place for the Holy Spirit of God.

We have already settled the theology of it: the Holy Spirit has sealed you permanently. At your salvation, He promised not only to come, but also to stay with you until you reach the glories of heaven. If you do not have the Spirit, you are not a real Christian:

> *And if anyone does not have the Spirit of Christ,*
> *they do not belong to Christ.* (Rom. 8:9, NIV)

When the Spirit—who lives in you—is offended, the Bible calls this "grieving" the Holy Spirit. If this happens, He does not leave your life, but He does stop filling your life. Examine this passage from several Bible translations to better understand this grieving.

> *And do not grieve the Holy Spirit of God [or "of-*
> *fend Him" or "make Him sad"], by whom you were*
> *sealed for the day of redemption.* (Eph. 4:30)

> *And do not bring sorrow to God's Holy Spirit by*
> *the way you live. Remember, he has identified you*
> *as his own, guaranteeing that you will be saved on*
> *the day of redemption.* (Eph. 4:30, NLT)

> *Don't give God's Holy Spirit any reason to be upset with*
> *you. He has put his seal on you for the day you will be set*
> *free from the world of sin.* (Eph. 4:30, GOD'S WORD)

This is the language of a strained relationship. It is like the Holy Spirit retreats to an inner room until you clean out the other rooms of your heart to give Him free rein. He will not *force* Himself upon you.

Remember, this relationship mirrors a marriage. In a marriage, biblically, a man and woman are married for life. Though they are bound together as one flesh, at times one spouse will grieve, upset, or make the other sad, resulting in a tense relationship. The marriage is still intact, the commitment is still strong, and life continues under one roof. But the relationship's harmony has been disturbed for a time.

The same is true of your relationship with the Holy Spirit. He is the honored guest of your life—in fact, not simply a guest but the Master of your life. But just as in a marriage, sinful things you think, say, and do upset this holy person. When offended, He does not leave, but He also does not fill you unless you live a life surrendered to holy living.

As the *Holy* Spirit, He only desires to dwell in a *holy* vessel. If we want Him to fully guide and empower our Christian walk and ministry, we have to do so on His terms. His terms not only include surrender, but they also include a lifestyle of holiness and righteousness that matches the standard of God's holy Word. There is no way around it: the Holy Spirit will only fully guide a holy person.

The Context: IN-filling after Rooting-OUT

The outline of Ephesians is simple:

> Chapters 1–3: Understanding the glory and purposes of God (Theology)
>
> Chapters 4–5: Living in a way that matches His purposes (Practice)

In the first half, Paul makes sure we understand that we belong to God completely as His children, including having the Spirit of God dwelling in us, never to leave. We have been authorized to live out God's purposes by the power of God. We are called to join in the story of God's plan that started before the foundation of the world and will be consummated in bringing all of creation under the Lordship of Jesus. We are not just disciples; we are servants of God's master plan.

The Pattern of Transformation

In the second half, Paul helps us know how to live a life that matches that amazing truth. Ephesians 4:17–5:21 clarifies the type of lifestyle that is worthy of the calling God has given you. It is the lifestyle that invites the Spirit to empower you. The filling of the Spirit (Eph. 5:18) is the culmination and the goal of the holy lifestyle pictured in these thiry-six verses. The pattern of holy living is introduced in the beginning of this section:

> *You were taught, with regard to your former way of life, to put off your old self, which is being corrupted by its deceitful desires; to be made new in the attitude of your minds; and to put on the new self, created to be like God in true righteousness and holiness.* (Eph. 4:22–24, NIV)

Here is the pattern:

1. **Put off** an old sin (sinful habit/practice) (Eph. 4:22)
2. **Renew your mind** (change how you think) (Eph. 4:23)
3. **Put on** the holy opposite (godly habit/practice) (Eph. 4:24)

All three practices are essential for life transformation. Observe the first example Paul gives in relationship to speaking truth (4:25):

1. **Put off** falsehood
2. **Renew your thinking** by realizing we are all members of the same body. No part of a body (a leg) would lie to another part (an arm). We are all one being.
3. Therefore, **put on** truth-speaking

The key to life transformation is not just putting off, or breaking, old habits. You must be intentional about replacing bad habits with new, holy habits. But for this to stick, your perspective must change. Your old sinful self might lie to someone else because he or she is not related to you. But if that person really is one with you—as close as one part of a body to another—you must be truthful. This is how the kingdom works.

Paul then gives more examples of sins to be put off, ways of thinking to be changed, and holy habits to be put on. The flow of this reasoning (Eph. 4:25–5:21) is as follows:

- **FALSEHOOD** (4:25) – Put off falsehood and put on truth
- **ANGER** (4:26–27) – Put off anger and be reconciled quickly
- **STEALING** (4:28) – Put off stealing and put on hard work and generosity
- **WRONG CONVERSATION** (4:29) – Put off corrupting talk and put on words that build up
- **HATRED** (4:31–32) – Put off anger and hatred and put on kindness and forgiveness
- [**INTERLUDE** (5:1–2) – Imitate God and walk in love]
- **SEXUAL IMPURITY AND COVETOUSNESS** (5:3–5) – Put off all sexual impurity, covetousness, and crude joking and put on a life of thanksgiving
- **DARK LIVING** (5:6–14) – Put off walking as children of darkness and put on walking as children of light, exposing all sin
- **UNWISE LIVING** (5:15–16) – Put off unwise living and put on making the best use of your time

- **FOOLISH LIVING** (5:17) – Put off foolishness and put on understanding the will of the Lord
- **DRUNKENNESS** (5:18–21) – Put off being filled with wine and put on being filled with the Spirit manifesting all of its outcomes

Ephesians 5:18 comes at the climax of this admonition to turn from sinful habits and live in a holy or righteous manner.

Vessels of Use for God

Do you long to see God move in your life? Do you hunger for Him to transform you? Do you yearn to be used by God in some great way? Do you aspire to make a difference in this world? Do you hope to see the Book of Acts reenacted around you?

If so, you must take the holiness path that Paul taught his child in Timothy. Paul admonished Timothy to present himself as a worker approved by God—the type of person God could use.

> *Do your best to present yourself to God as one approved, a worker who has no need to be ashamed, rightly handling the word of truth.* (2 Tim. 2:15)

As with Ephesians 5:18, 2 Timothy 2:15 must be set in context. In this chapter, Paul encouraged Timothy to be a strong soldier of Christ. He was called to make disciples who could make disciples (2 Tim. 2:2), but Paul reminded him that this ministry would only bear fruit as he endured the hardship of this path (2 Tim. 2:3ff).

Second, Paul reminded him that it will not only be *hard*, but the servant of God must be *holy*. All of us are called to be servants of God. We must not only learn the ministry skills that come with our calling, but we must *endure hardship* and *embrace holiness*.

Embracing holiness means becoming a holy vessel. We must depart from all iniquity. Without fleeing old sinful patterns, we are unfit for God's use.

> *Now in a great house there are not only vessels of gold and silver but also of wood and clay, some for honorable use, some for dishonorable. Therefore, if anyone cleanses himself from what is dishonorable, he will be a vessel for honorable use, set apart as holy, useful to the master of the house, ready for every good work. So flee youthful passions and pursue righteousness, faith, love, and peace, along with those who call on the Lord from a pure heart.* (2 Tim. 2:20–22)

Cultural tolerance of sin isn't new. In fact, it has frequently spiraled out of control in various cultures throughout the ages. It has been the repeated pattern since the fall of humanity:

> *And since they did not see fit to acknowledge God, God gave them up to a debased mind to do what ought not to be done. They were filled with all manner of unrighteousness, evil, covetousness, malice. They are full of envy, murder, strife,*

> *deceit, maliciousness. They are gossips, slanderers, haters of God, insolent, haughty, boastful, inventors of evil, disobedient to parents, foolish, faithless, heartless, ruthless. Though they know God's righteous decree that those who practice such things deserve to die, **they not only do them but give approval to those who practice them**.* (Rom. 1:28–32, emphasis added)

To become a holy vessel, you must agree with God about His standard of righteousness rather than succumbing to society's ever-changing standards of right and wrong.

Before Paul explained about being a holy vessel, he reminded Timothy of the theology behind his admonition:

> *But God's firm foundation stands, bearing this seal: "The Lord knows those who are his," and, "Let everyone who names the name of the Lord depart from iniquity."* (2 Tim. 2:19)

The Lord knows who His own children are. When you give your life to Christ you are sealed in Him forever—you will never lose your place as a son or daughter of the King. But the King wants His children to "depart from iniquity." To be approved by God for usefulness in life and ministry, you must live a holy lifestyle as a holy vessel. To be entrusted with some significant work, whether in your family, your school, your workplace, or the ends of the earth, you must choose the path of holy living. An honorable vessel is one that has fled from all sinful passions and instead clings to holy habits.

Today's culture has not changed God's standard of right and wrong. When believers conform to the world rather than the Word, they experience a great lack of the presence of God. The Holy Spirit is noticeably absent. Such absence only compounds bondage to sin and shame.

The reality is that people—even believers—sin because it is enjoyable for a while. It is the pill that is sweet in the mouth and bitter in the stomach (see Prov. 5:3–4). We love that brief rush of doing it our way, of indulging our flesh, of letting our minds race where they want, of getting revenge on someone who has hurt us, of saying whatever we want, and so on. When we pursue these passions that we have had since our youth, the sweet pill turns to bitterness. Destructive repercussions abound.

And even when we choose the path of holiness, we live around people—even fellow believers—who indulge in and celebrate questionable or sinful practices. Perhaps you cower from saying anything. You would be frowned upon or ridiculed in our current culture for abstaining from the same banter or not going along with the crowd, much less speaking up that such behavior is not fit for a child of God. Such silence quietly condones the decline in values among Christians.

Again, we have sinned because we have not done what we ought to have done—call our friends back to a higher standard.

Does this pattern sound familiar to you? We dabble, or even indulge, in sin (thus condoning sin) every day of the week. But, for one hour on Sundays, we dress ourselves up, don masks of "holiness," and ask God to bless us.

Perhaps you feel that is true of many other believers, but not normally of you. You are a committed, sincere follower of Jesus. Yet how often do you yourself indulge in thoughts, words and actions that don't conform to the Word and still expect God to bless the rest of your life and ministry? Are there areas of your life that you would be embarrassed to show in the light of day? Do you have thought processes that you know do not honor God?

If so, you may not be gorging your appetite on the feasts of iniquity, but you are still picking at the dessert tray of sin.

You must abandon any indulgence of sin and instead indulge in righteousness. When God's people choose the enduring delights of righteousness over the passing delights of temptation, revival is the result.

Every Revival Is a Refining Movement

Just as societies have spiraled downward with their approval of sinful lifestyles, so also revivals and awakenings have called believers back to God's standard of righteousness. Most revivals in history have taken the holiness journey of Ephesians 4:17–5:21. Each started as a *sin confession*

> MOST REVIVALS IN HISTORY HAVE **TAKEN THE HOLINESS JOURNEY OF EPHESIANS** 4:17–5:21

movement to God personally, and sometimes corporately. Whenever God's children have purged themselves from delighting in sin, God has been delighted to fill them with His Spirit.

In many historical revivals, a pattern emerges. First God raises up a servant (or group of servants) who calls His people back to Himself from the midst of a wicked culture. Together, they expectantly wait on the Most High in prayer, actively seeking Him, unsure of how He will show up. Most revivals then move to a point of individual conviction of sin and personal confession to God to seek forgiveness.

Some (though not all) of these revivals go a step further. A bold individual will venture out from behind his mask of holiness (like the ones we all wear) to confess sin in his life to the larger group. This confession goes beyond the normal protocols of confessing sin only to a person offended. Rather, this person confesses to a larger group in order to expose sin's dreadful hold, to break its control over their lives.

And then the moment of truth arises. If the group receives that confession with compassion, forgiveness, and honor for the confessor's vulnerability, a chain reaction may emerge. If not, the flicker of a budding revival is blown out. But when the response is compassionate, frequently another saint will follow the same example, and then another. Some revivals in history have started with days or weeks of God's children publicly confessing their sin, seeking forgiveness, and being restored to God and to each other.[10]

The goal is not to confess sin or flaunt sinful ways; the goal is to draw close to God. When we want God more than sin, we venture from behind the masks of uprightness and choose the path of vulnerability and transparency. Revivals in history are so rare because God's children prefer the pleasures of sin (and hiding its hold on their lives) over the refining path of righteousness (and any embarrassment they feel in acknowledging their past).

> *And this is the judgment: the light has come into the world, and **people loved the darkness** rather than the light because their works were evil. **For everyone who does wicked things hates the light and does not come to the light, lest his works should be exposed.** But whoever does what is true comes to the light, so that it may be clearly seen that his works have been carried out in God.* (John 3:19–21, emphasis added)

At this point in your life, do you prefer the passing delights of sin more than the enduring delight of holiness? Do you prefer the comfortable shadows of darkness to the discomforting exposure of the light?

---

10 This is not a license for flaunting of sins in public, boasting about sin, or confessing sins that would cause damage in the group. Such a practice does more harm than good. Sound judgment must be used. Again, not all revivals are public confession movements—so don't press this aspect. God's Spirit will dictate how a revival manifests itself.

When God's children…

- *allow His Word to shine into the crevices of their souls*
- *and humble themselves under the conviction of the Holy Spirit*
- *and allow a holy fear to seize them*
- *and bravely shed their "everything is okay" masks*
- *and confess their sins in a community that aspires to holiness*
- *and such sharing is received with love, acceptance, and forgiveness*
- *and it produces an even greater sense of reverential awe*
- *and prompts others in the community to follow suit*
- *and this chain reaction causes the group to humble themselves to seek God above all else, hungering for Him, surrendering to Him*

…then revival begins to break out among His people. They are awakened!

This pattern has occurred repeatedly throughout history, in groups and in individuals.

And yet we want shortcuts. We cry out for revival—personally and corporately—but we lack the courage to take the path that leads there. No awakening emerges without the deeply refining process of confession. Confession and surrender are the crucibles of revival.

There is no other path. And so revival—true revival—is rare.

Revival in your life, in your church, and in your ministry awaits these conditions: absolute surrender to God's mission and complete rooting out of sin personally and corporately.

Avoid the Scent of Sin

A shocking practice among disciples of Jesus today is to see how close we can get to the line of temptation without crossing into sin. In addition, our consciences become increasingly numb to sinful images, thoughts, or actions that would have shocked us earlier in our Christian walk. What's more, the children of God dabble in every type of sin while at the same time convincing themselves that dabbling is not the same thing as actually sinning. Believers in our society flirt with temptation and allow the stench of hints of sin to scent their garments. As consciences become more hardened, in the spirit of the downward spiral of Romans 1, believers begin condoning lifestyles they would have frowned upon earlier (Rom. 1:32).

The proper emphasis of a holy lifestyle is not to see *how close* to the line between temptation and sin that you can get, but how far from that line you can remain. Though there is a line between temptation and sin, when you *contemplate* temptation in your heart, have you not already sinned? Why would you even *want* to try to draw close to that line?

The point of a holy lifestyle is **to avoid sin in your life** so that you both live holy and also avoid any appearance (scent) of dabbling in sin. The Holy Spirit only fills a believer who actively roots out sin and attempts to stay away from any hint of sin. Yet it is easy for us to rationalize away the magnitude of sin, thinking, "We live in a completely different culture than the one Paul described two thousand years ago. Sin is too accepted in our society. I would be shunned to have such holy standards."

Yet the city of Ephesus was a demonic stronghold, the global center of the worship of the idol Artemis and a den of unparalleled sexual license. The believers in Ephesus could easily rationalize that these alternate lifestyles or accepted social mores were just the way it was. How easy for them to be tainted by such sin.

But listen to the strong language Paul used in a corrupt city. The standard he upholds is not merely avoiding sin but staying as far away from it as possible:

> *But sexual immorality and all impurity or covetousness* **must not even be named among you,** *as is proper among saints.... **For it is shameful even to speak of the things** that they do in secret.* (Eph. 5:3, 12, emphasis added)

Paul is not saying that you should not confess sin; that is essential. What is shameful is to talk in a cavalier way about the things people do in secret. It is shameful to let our minds speculate on the details of sinful practices. How often do believers joke about sins or share lurid details?

We should do exactly the opposite: flee from even naming the sinful things done in secret and avoid sin in our lives.

Above Reproach

Another way to state this spiritual principle is that we should be above reproach. All Christian leaders should live by this standard, and they should be an example to all Jesus-followers:

> *For an overseer, as God's steward, must be **above reproach**.* (Titus 1:7, emphasis added; see also 1 Tim. 3:2)

To be above reproach means that you not only avoid sin, but you avoid even *giving the appearance of sin*. Other translations express this as having a blameless life or a good reputation so people should not be able to say you live in a wrong way.

For instance, a Christian leader should not only avoid getting involved in a sinful relationship with someone of the opposite sex. To be above reproach, he should also avoid ever putting himself into a situation where he would be tempted to become sexually involved OR could even give the perception to others that he might be in such a relationship. To be above reproach, he would take necessary precautions. For example, he would avoid meeting alone with a woman in his office, and perhaps refuse to ride alone with a woman in a car.

Today, such precautions may be perceived as overkill. But such actions not only help you avoid sin, but help you stay far away from temptation. When you live this way, it is hard for anyone to lay blame on (or reproach) you by the appearances of your life. In other words, do not only resist temptation but avoid situations where you could be compromised or sin could be suspected by others.

Just as the smell of smoke lingers on clothing when someone has been near it, so the stench of sin lingers on your life when you dabble with or even contemplate it. Rid yourself from any scent of sin—in your thoughts, words, and actions.

The Fragrance of Surrender to God

Ultimately, the reason we want to live free of sin is to imitate God, taking on the sweet fragrance of surrender (Eph. 4:17–5:21).

> *Therefore be imitators of God, as beloved children. And walk in love, as Christ loved us and gave himself up for us, a fragrant offering and sacrifice to God.* (Eph. 5:1–2)

The center of this amazing passage is that we are to imitate no one less than God Himself. He is our Father and we are His beloved children. Jesus lived that type of life—one of surrender—and wafted the fragrance of an offering to God. His lifestyle carried no scent of sin, no hint of wrongdoing. To imitate God is to imitate His Son. When we do, our lives, like Jesus's, give off a fragrant aroma—the aroma of surrendering ourselves to God.

In the S.W.A.P. progression, "S," "W," and "A" are all parts of the same process. We root out sin because we surrender to God. And we surrender to God so that we can imitate Him and live free from the pervasive stench of sin. Sometimes this process takes a good deal of waiting on God—waiting for Him to change our desires.

Pure, Undivided Devotion

Here again, our analogy of marriage can help. Imagine a couple standing at the altar. They have written their own vows to each other. The bride says to the husband: "I vow to be true to you 364 days of the year."

Would the husband be pleased to have her devotion most of the year knowing that she would be untrue to him a small percentage of the time—just one day a year? What would he do? He would walk out of the ceremony and not return to the altar until his bride has decided to be devoted to him only—365 days a year.

The husband wants all of or none of her.

But as part of the bride of Christ, do you do the same thing? Dabbling in sin, entertaining it, and enjoying just a little bit of it in your life is no different than telling your Beloved you are committed to Him 364 days of the year. That is not surrender. That is not holiness. He is not pleased by that offer.

Instead, your goal in this marriage to Jesus should be to discern (to understand) what is pleasing to Him.

Try to discern what is pleasing to the Lord. Take no part in the unfruitful works of darkness, but instead expose them. (Eph. 5:10–11)

God is calling you to a fresh, deeper desire to live as a holy servant of the Most High. He is calling you to live in a pleasing way with your Beloved one hundred percent of the time. He is calling you to value intimacy with Him over the passing pleasures of sin.

As you do, the Spirit of the Most High will delight in taking residence in such a holy vessel. This is the lifestyle you are called to.

None of us ever lives completely free from sin. But our goal should be to grow more and more inclined to live uprightly than to wander into sin.

Expose Sin and Receive Forgiveness

The good news is that your Savior is not only ready to forgive you in providing salvation, but is ready to forgive you each day you sin. Your Holy God is the God of love. He is the loving Father ever ready to receive His kids who wander off.

Though your goal is a lifestyle as free from sin as possible, to get there you must consistently root out sin—confess it and receive forgiveness, sin by sin. Some of these sins you are all too aware of. Some are strongholds that have plagued you for years. Others are sins you are not even aware of, but the Convictor can help you become aware of them at the right time.

To please the Lord, you must take no part in the works of darkness, rather expose them (Eph. 5:11). The natural response to sin in your life is to hide the ones you are aware of and ignore the ones you are not aware of.

The enemy is whispering in your ear constantly:

- "That one's not really so bad; you don't need to confess it to God."
- "Don't tell anyone else about this. Keep the mask on."
- "Wouldn't you be ashamed if people knew about this? Better not to say anything."
- "You can conquer this one on your own. No need for help from others."
- "Everyone else is doing it. It must be okay. Times have changed."
- "Go ahead and do it one more time. God will forgive you again."

Stop listening to the enticing lies of the adversary. The way to live a Spirit-filled life is the very opposite of what the devil is telling you: expose sin so that you can live a holy lifestyle that is fit for the infilling Holy Spirit. Your sinful, fallen tendency is to let sin remain in the darkness. God's solution is to shine the spotlight of His Word on it. Expose it. All sins need to be exposed and confessed to God. Confession is agreeing with God about what He says is sin. It's admitting your fault and guilt.

CONFESSION IS AGREEING WITH GOD ABOUT WHAT HE SAYS IS SIN. **IT'S ADMITTING YOUR FAULT AND GUILT.**

Typically, if you continue to stumble into temptation, and are unable to find victory over it, the time has come to confess it to holy friends who can help you. While many of your sins can be confessed and forgiven in the privacy of your heart, some sins can only be overcome by exposing them to other trusted friends who can help you overcome them.

The Arduous Journey of Rooting Out Sin

The process of letting the Word of God expose your sins, confessing them, receiving forgiveness, and putting on holy opposites is the process of rooting out sin. This process can be painful in the beginning, but is always joyful in the end.

The "W" and the "A" of S.W.A.P. are intimately intertwined. To work through this process involves <u>W</u>aiting on God in prayer. This is a time not only for you to <u>S</u>urrender to God and to discern His purposes, but to give the shining light of the Holy Spirit time to expose sin in your life.

He wants unhurried time with you: to expose sin, for you to show remorse and confess it, to be forgiven of it and to be free from it. It is an arduous journey, but He is the Spirit of your gentle, loving Father. He will not overwhelm you beyond what you can bear.

To be filled with the Spirit, you will have to embark on the journey of letting every sin in your life be rooted out. The shining light the Spirit uses is regular reading of and meditating on the whole of God's Word. There God can show you His standards to for your life.

Do you really want to be free of sin? If so, you are ready to start this journey. When you ask the Holy Spirit, He will convict you of sin; it is one of His main roles:

> *And when he comes, he will convict the world concerning sin and righteousness and judgment.* (John 16:8)

As you read your Bible, lay your heart before the Lord and ask Him to shine His spotlight in your heart. In the pages of the Scripture you will encounter a God who calls you to a holy standard and who also demonstrates amazing love to forgive you and draw you close to Himself.

Choose the way that is everlasting.

> *Search me, O God, and know my heart!*
> *Try me and know my thoughts!*
> *And see if there be any grievous way in me,*
> *and lead me in the way everlasting!* (Ps. 139:23–24)

Exposing Sin

Before the digital era, rolls of film were loaded in the back of cameras. When the film roll was finished, you would wind it up into the small canister it was housed in, open the back flap of the camera, take it out, and bring it to a photo developer. On a number of occasions, I have had the agonizing tragedy of opening the back of the camera *before* the film was wound completely into its canister. When that happens, every square inch of film that is exposed to light literally becomes light. Photos developed from these frames are solid white.

> *But when anything is exposed by the light, it becomes visible,*
> *for anything that becomes visible is light. Therefore it says,*
> *"Awake, O sleeper,*
> *and arise from the dead,*
> *and Christ will shine on you." (Eph. 5:13–14)*

Confessing sin to God, and sometimes to others, brings an amazing miracle. Dark things become light! When anything is exposed by the light it becomes visible, and anything that becomes visible is light. Do you long to live a holy and pure life? Then you must expose sin and flood it with light.

> *But if we walk in the light, as he is in the light, we have fel-*
> *lowship with one another, and the blood of Jesus his Son*
> *cleanses us from all sin. If we say we have no sin, we deceive*
> *ourselves, and the truth is not in us. If we confess our sins, he*

> *is faithful and just to forgive us our sins and to cleanse us from*
> *all unrighteousness. If we say we have not sinned, we make*
> *him a liar, and his word is not in us.* (1 John 1:7–10)

Rather than walk in the dishonesty of darkness, we are called to run in light to our Father to be cleansed from our sins.

But exposing and being forgiven of sin is just the first step. It is like breaking the chains of bondage. To stay holy, you must put on the holy opposite, and this includes removing sources of temptation when possible. To remain sober, no alcoholic would keep alcohol in his or her home. The temptation is too great. You must flee sin *and* you must flee sinful situations.

Listen to these words from Paul to his colleague in the ministry:

> *So flee youthful passions and pursue righteous-*
> *ness, faith, love, and peace, along with those who call*
> *on the Lord from a pure heart.* (2 Tim. 2:22)

Listen to these words from Jesus to His faithful disciples:

> *And if your hand causes you to sin, cut it off. It is better for you*
> *to enter life crippled than with two hands to go to hell, to the*
> *unquenchable fire. And if your foot causes you to sin, cut it off.*
> *It is better for you to enter life lame than with two feet to be*
> *thrown into hell. And if your eye causes you to sin, tear it out.*

It is better for you to enter the kingdom of God with one eye than with two eyes to be thrown into hell. (Mark 9:43–47)

Jesus calls you to remove frequent stumbling blocks in your life that haul you down to hell rather than lift you up to the light.

Part of what I do in my forty-day times with God is sit before Him with an open Bible. I pull out my journal and let Him identify sins in my life. I try not to argue with Him or reason them away. I write these down, confess them to Him, express sorrow for having offended Him, and ask His forgiveness. If there are other people I need to get right with, I commit to doing that at the first opportunity. If He exposes a sin that I need confess to someone else in order to be free from its hold, I must obey.

Peeling the Layers of the Onion–From the Inside

When our three sons were young, I had been working hard to conquer the sin of selfishness. Year after year, I worked hard to root out selfishness in my life. At that time, God gave me an image of my sin; it was like the layers of an onion. Each year, I would peel back a layer of selfishness, thinking I had finally conquered it. But there is nothing like having children to help you realize how selfish you can be. Just when I thought I had conquered selfishness, God would reveal a deeper form of it in my life—another layer of the onion of that sin.

Time went by, and finally, I thought there were no more layers of selfishness to peel off. But an incident one day with my children showed me that selfishness was still rooted in the deep places of my heart. My heart grew heavy as I realized that I was still peeling back more layers of the onion.

The next day in my quiet time, God altered the image of the onion in my mind. I had the imagery all wrong. When you peel an onion from the outside, you can see it getting smaller and smaller until it is gone. But the truer reality was that I was on the inside of the onion, peeling off layer by layer, with no idea how big the onion truly was! It was an overwhelming image.

I walked in a depressed state for two days, mourning the depth of my sin. But our God is a life-giving God. He convicts us to bring life, not death. He used that image to call me to a deeper hunger for righteousness that goes to the core of my being. I want to live a life of integrity. Integrity is being true through and through.

Jesus talked about various layers of the same sin. In the Sermon on the Mount, He pointed to deeper, subtler versions of the same sins. He introduced each of these sins with the phrase "You have heard it said _____, but I say to you _____."

For instance, "You have heard it said, 'Do not murder,' but I say to you, do not be angry" (paraphrased). Whether it was anger, lust, divorce, taking oaths, or hating enemies,

Jesus emphasized that sins have many layers to them and we must never become proud of our perceived righteousness (Matt. 5:21–48).

None of us will become perfect before we see Jesus face to face. The onions of sin in our lives can be quite large. God wants us to continue to peel back layers of sin so that we become more and more like Jesus. He wants us to be true through and through. If

GOD WANTS US TO CONTINUE TO PEEL BACK LAYERS OF SIN **SO THAT WE BECOME MORE AND MORE LIKE JESUS.**

we are rooting out sin, pride, lust, anger, or lying, let us root them out completely in all their various subtleties.

Never become proud and assume you have finally conquered sin. The Holy Spirit will keep humbling you, if you will let Him, to realize that you still have more to confess. But in His graciousness, He will not burden you beyond what you can bear. He is loving and gentle with you. Let Him expose sin in each layer of its hold on you. Demonstrate true sorrow and resolve to live differently. Allow Him to bring forgiveness and restoration to you as His son or daughter. Ask Him to help you put on the holy opposite and invite His Spirit to fill you.

At all times, remember that you cannot earn His favor through this process. As a child, you already have His favor. So come to Him as a child comes to a loving Father, not as a slave to a harsh taskmaster. No sin in your life will separate you from that eternal relationship.

For I am sure that neither death nor life, nor angels nor rulers, nor things present nor things to come, nor powers, nor height nor depth, nor anything else in all creation, will be able to separate us from the love of God in Christ Jesus our Lord. (Rom. 8:38-39)

Honesty in the Family

The confession of sin and the restoration that follows—the forgiveness process—is therefore a family process. Your Father deals compassionately with you as His child, so you always have confidence to come to Him. His standards are firm but His forgiveness is boundless. A critical element in this family is honesty.

In raising our three sons, we had to make choices about which offenses incurred what degree of discipline. Our sons knew that, in addition to insubordination, the greatest offense they could commit in the family was lying. Falsehood could undermine every other issue we wanted to help the boys conquer. If they could not be honest about other wrongdoings, then they could not confront them and mature into the men God wanted them to be.

Even at a young age, our boys could distinguish between the severity of punishments they would get for various offenses. Hitting one's brother warranted a much lighter punishment than lying. Plus, if we caught a boy lying, he received not only that punishment but also the one that matched the actual offense.

I recall a moment in which one of the boys complained that his older brother hit him. When I asked the older brother if this was true, I could see the wheels turning in his mind. Even at a young age, he was calculating the cost of each punishment, especially if caught lying. (And parents seem to always know when their kids are lying, right?) I had to suppress a laugh as he chose not to hide his wrongdoing. "Yes, sir! I hit him." In doing so, he chose to confront the sin and receive the punishment for it, along with the restoration that followed.

Even today, our three sons who are grown men still value honesty as a core value in our family. No matter what is going on, we are honest with each other. Only then can we make progress.

What was the first sin recorded in the early church in the Book of Acts? Lying! Ananias and his wife Sapphira lied about how much they sold a piece of property for and what percentage of it they were giving to the church. When they were confronted about it and lied in response, God struck both of them dead:

> *But Peter said, "Ananias, why has Satan filled your heart to lie to the Holy Spirit and to keep back for yourself part of the proceeds of the land? While it remained unsold, did it not remain your own? And after it was sold, was it not at your disposal? Why is it that you have contrived this deed in your heart? You have not lied to man but to God." (Acts 5:3–4)*

Such a punishment in the era of the new covenant—in the church of Jesus Christ—seems harsh to us. But it appears that God wanted to reinforce with His children (1) that He would not tolerate sin in the church and (2) that any sin could be dealt with *if* the brothers and sisters were honest with each other and with God. Your Father can forgive and heal anything in your life if you are honest about it. Without honesty, you cannot confront the issues and grow into the man, woman, or church God designed you to be. Always choose honesty, no matter the consequence.

Sweet Restoration

Walking in the light, or walking in holiness, is essential for the Spirit Walk. It starts with honesty about our sin, which leads to sweet restoration: confessing that sin is sin, asking forgiveness, and receiving the words "My child, I forgive you" from the lips of our Father. Think of the purest, most loving, most compassionate father you can and multiply it by one thousand. That is a dim glimpse of how amazing your heavenly Daddy is. His arms are stretched wide to receive you in the embrace of forgiveness. There is no sin you can confess that He will not forgive, forget, and then cleanse from you.

His Son took every one of your sins upon Him on the cross. His sacrifice was enough to bring you complete forgiveness and restoration.

Once again, remember, your relationship with God is similar to a marriage. My wife and I do not have a lot of disagreements, but they do come occasionally. When tensions arise in our marriage—perhaps one of us offends the other—it is simply that: tensions in a marriage. The marriage is still intact. The marriage vows are still in place. That is *never* in question. It's just that we might not be getting along too well right at that moment.

During disagreements, we are still fully committed to the other, but we're just angry or hurt at that moment. Neither of us ever uses the word "divorce." Never. We decided that before we got engaged. We are committed to each other for life. We are committed to making the relationship beautiful. Therefore, we always find a way to make every disagreement result in restoration—and as quickly as possible. The repentance process usually starts with one (or both simultaneously) confessing to the other, "I was wrong to do _____. Would you forgive me?" We are committed to forgiving, forgetting, and restoring. Though the previous tension was painful, the restoration is sweet. We keep no list of wrongs and harbor no grudges. We seek an honest and harmonious relationship at all times because we value *intimacy*.

God wants to be intimate with you and wants to evidence this by giving you the fullness of the Spirit who indwells you. Since the Holy Spirit is a person and sin grieves Him, He will retreat like any partner in a marriage when offended. Unlike earthly marriage, however, He is never in the wrong. You always are the one who offends Him. Though He retreats from filling your life, He whispers, and sometimes shouts, for you to return. He is ready to receive you and fill you again, if you will depart from sin.

Few experiences compare with the intimacy that comes from being honest about an offense, expressing sorrow, asking for forgiveness, and seeking restoration of the relationship—whether with a spouse, a family member, or a friend. The same is true with God. God loves to fill you with His Spirit as a sign of being restored. God is not an evil Father, purposefully holding back His Spirit from His children. Rather, He longs to give you the gift of the Spirit.

> *What father among you, if his son asks for a fish, will instead of a fish give him a serpent; or if he asks for an egg, will give him a scorpion? If you then, who are evil, know how to give good gifts to your children, how much more will the heavenly Father give the Holy Spirit to those who ask him!"* (Luke 11:11–13)

Being filled with the Spirit is not elusive. It is not magical. It does not require special formulas or incantations. God is not reluctant to pour out His Spirit. Just the opposite. All He expects is for His children to seek Him in humility, surrender, and confess. You must long for intimacy with Him—but it's intimacy on His terms.

The Life-Giving Power of Confession

As God highlights sin in your life through the pages of Scripture, you must understand the essential difference between the conviction of the Holy Spirit and the condemnation of the devil. **God convicts; Satan condemns. God's conviction brings hope. The devil's condemnation destroys hope.**

> *The thief comes only to steal and kill and destroy. I [Jesus] came that they may have life and have it abundantly.* (John 10:10)

God points out sin in order that you might have abundant life. The enemy points out sin in order to pull you down and destroy you. God gives life. Satan takes life.

You must also understand **the essential difference between the conviction of sin by the Holy Spirit and the commendation of sin by the devil.** If the devil cannot get condemnation to work in your life, he will start commending your practice of sin. While conviction (by the Spirit) results in remorse and a desire to change, commendation by the devil results in excusing your sin—"it's not so bad after all." **God's conviction brings life-giving change. The devil's commendation brings bondage-building license.**

As you work through sins, if you hear words of condemnation—words that tear you down and give you no hope—those are not from the Holy Spirit. If you hear words that pat you on the back and tell you sin is not so bad, those are not from the Holy Spirit either. The Holy Spirit's convicting words illuminated by the shining light of the Bible can be painful, but they always bring the hope that things can be better. It is the pain of a surgeon's healing scalpel, not an assassin's deadly dagger.

> *For the word of God is living and active, sharper than any two-edged sword, piercing to the division of soul and of spirit, of joints and of marrow, and discerning the thoughts and intentions of the heart. And no creature is hidden from his sight, but all are naked and exposed to the eyes of him to whom we must give account.* (Heb. 4:12–13)

The Wesleyan (Methodist) movement began as small groups started to examine their own hearts to see if they were living a holy lifestyle. To foster this process, they reviewed a list of common sins each week so they could quickly seek the forgiveness of God and others. This list facilitated accountability within the group to seek intimacy with God.

1. Am I consciously or unconsciously creating the impression that I am better than I really am? In other words, am I a hypocrite?
2. Am I honest in all my acts and words, or do I exaggerate?
3. Do I confidentially pass on to others what has been said to me in confidence?
4. Can I be trusted?

5. Am I a slave to dress, friends, work, or habits?
6. Am I self-conscious, self-pitying, or self-justifying?
7. Did the Bible live in me today?
8. Do I give the Bible time to speak to me every day?
9. Am I enjoying prayer?
10. When did I last speak to someone else of my faith?
11. Do I pray about the money I spend?
12. Do I get to bed on time and get up on time?
13. Do I disobey God in anything?
14. Do I insist upon doing something about which my conscience is uneasy?
15. Am I defeated in any part of my life?
16. Am I jealous, impure, critical, irritable, touchy, or distrustful?
17. How do I spend my spare time?
18. Am I proud?
19. Do I thank God that I am not as other people, especially as the Pharisees who despised the publican?
20. Is there anyone whom I fear, dislike, disown, criticize, hold resentment toward, or disregard? If so, what am I doing about it?
21. Do I grumble or complain constantly?
22. Is Christ real to me?

Many groups have used this list or one similar to it. But the standard they all point to is the Word of God. Many frequently add one more question at the end: "Were you truthful about your answers?"

Rather than moving into a legalistic form of Christianity dominated by dos and don'ts, your goal is to move into a living relationship with the Word of God where God helps you live up to His standards—to imitate Him. The God of Grace is not waiting to slap your hands with a ruler for every rule you break. Rather, He is wooing you into a relationship where you *want* to be a better person because you want to *please* Him. Living in relationship with Him and His Word makes you want to live like Him.

Ask God to show you your sins, whether you were previously aware of them or not. Confess them to Him and ask His forgiveness. Confession is like a muscle. The more you use it, the stronger it will become in your life. Form a habit of quickly confessing sin to God and others

> CONFESSION IS LIKE A MUSCLE. **THE MORE YOU USE IT, THE STRONGER IT WILL BECOME IN YOUR LIFE.**

and immediately seeking forgiveness. There are few joys greater than confessing sin and being restored in relationship. All of God's interactions with you—even the difficult ones—are life-giving. Where sin abounds, grace abounds even more!

Where sin increased, grace abounded all the more. (Rom. 5:20)

Forty-Days and Frequent Forays

Rooting out sin can follow the same rhythm as forty-day times (SWAPmeets) and frequent forays (quiet time). A SWAPmeet is a time to take several days to let God shine His light deeply in your soul, which includes illuminating sin.

Such unhurried times of letting God do a deep cleaning—a spring cleaning as it were—can be difficult but so wonderfully refreshing! These are precious times to journal what God shows you, not only of your sin but also of His words of affirmation and forgiveness. Remember, His conviction brings life.

In addition, your daily quiet times should be an occasion to let Him root out any recent, fresh sins. If SWAPmeets allow for a spring cleaning, quiet times provide daily tidying. You want to keep your accounts of offenses short with God. Let your conscience be clean before God.

> *"So I always take pains to have a clear conscience toward both God and man."* (Acts 24:16)

> *The aim of our charge is love that issues from a pure heart and a good conscience and a sincere faith.* (1 Tim. 1:5)

> *Let us draw near with a true heart in full assurance of faith, with our hearts sprinkled clean from an evil conscience and our bodies washed with pure water.* (Heb. 10:22)

Never consciously harbor any sin in your heart; confess quickly and often. Develop a rhythm in your life for longer periods of time to deep clean by rooting out sin, and use daily getaways to make sure you stay tidy with God.

Confess as Wide as the Offense

When God convicts you of sin, you must confess this sin at least as widely as the offense that was given. Some sins are between you and God; they are confessed to God alone. But others require a wider audience for confession. It's important to think through the right approach for confessing each individual sin.

Here are two general guidelines for how widely to confess sin:

First, make confession to anyone who has been offended by your sin.

Before you can come clean with God in worship, you must come clean with someone you have offended. If you have reason to believe that someone has been hurt or offended by a word, attitude, action, or inaction on your part, it is your responsibility to take the first step to confess your sin to that person or persons, ask forgiveness and right any wrong (make restitution if needed). As widely as your offense has hurt others is how widely you should confess your sin. You must confess to all within the circle of offense.

For example, I teach and train in many contexts. Over time I have had several embarrassing moments when I significantly erred with my words in front of large groups of people. After God convicted me of this, I had to return to that group and confess publicly that I was wrong.

This holds true even if you have been offended as well. Even if that person or group is ninety-nine percent at fault and you are only one percent at fault, it is still your responsibility to take the first step toward reconciliation.

However, you must be careful here. It might be foolhardy to confess certain sins to some people. Can you imagine how harmful it could be for a man to confess to a woman his impure thoughts about her? That would do more to damage than to help. The best course of action in this instance would be to bring impure thoughts to trusted, same-sex believers who would aid in accountability. Paul encourages Timothy to do this very thing with those who call on the Lord from a pure heart:

> *So flee youthful passions and pursue righteousness, faith,*
> *love, and peace, **along with** those who call on the Lord*
> *from a pure heart.* (2 Tim. 2:22, emphasis added)

> *So if you are offering your gift at the altar and there remember that your brother has something against you, leave your gift there before the altar and go. First be reconciled to your brother, and then come and offer your gift.* (Matt. 5:23–24)

You must review each sin one by one to determine your course of action.

Second, confess your sin to accountability partners when necessary to bring you victory over your sin.

Many sins will be confessed between you and God, others will be brought to those you offended. Sometimes, though, God will instruct you to confess some sins to other brothers or sisters who are pursuing a holy lifestyle. This helps expose these sins to the light and robs much of the power these sins hold over you. This process may free you from the bondage of sin, allowing these brothers or sisters to help you walk in a new way of life.

Allowing others to support you does not indicate weakness. You may have strongholds in your life that simply cannot be overcome alone. You were made to live in community. You need the body of Christ to help you bear these burdens, while you help bear theirs.

> *Brothers, if anyone is caught in any transgression, you who are spiritual should restore him in a spirit of gentleness. Keep watch on yourself, lest you too be tempted. Bear one another's burdens, and so fulfill the law of Christ.* (Gal. 6:1–2)

Many sins need to be confessed to a group of people who will love you and help you walk in holiness, for true healing to take place.

> *Therefore, confess your sins to one another and pray for one another, that you may be healed. The prayer of a righteous person has great power as it is working.* (James 5:16)

Confessing sin to another takes away the sting of sin and robs it of the power that it has in the darkness. Bringing sin to light with a

CONFESSING SIN TO ANOTHER **TAKES AWAY THE STING OF SIN** AND **ROBS IT OF THE POWER THAT IT HAS IN THE DARKNESS.**

group of trusted friends is often half the battle over sin. Now you can move from shame into the light of a healthy community that spurs you on to holy living.

Take care, brothers, lest there be in any of you an evil, unbelieving heart, leading you to fall away from the living God. But exhort one another every day, as long as it is called "today," that none of you may be hardened by the deceitfulness of sin. (Heb. 3:12–13)

And let us consider how to stir up one another to love and good works, not neglecting to meet together, as is the habit of some, but encouraging one another, and all the more as you see the Day drawing near. (Heb. 10:24–25)

The reoccurrence of the same sins in your life is a good indicator that you need to turn to a group for account- ability. When personal rooting out of sin does not appear to be conquering it, you need the help of a same-sex accountability group or partner.

To be successful however, accountability groups need several foundational values:

1. They, too, long for a pure and holy life.
2. They do not condone sin. They will not pat you on the back and say, "Oh, well. That's all right. We all do that." They, too, are horrified at sin and its effects.
3. They can keep confidence and do not share out- side the circle what you have shared.

4. They empathize with you, accept you, and help restore you because they love you unconditionally.
5. They choose to regularly ask you about your progress over sin and help you through the rough patches of temptation at any time of day or night.
6. They are brutally honest with each other; transparency is critical.
7. Their accountability is mutual—all members share with each other.

Accountability groups only work if you allow them to—you can deceive your group of trusted friends and hide yourself from them. You must want the righteous lifestyle of Jesus more than you want the pleasures of sin. If so, then an accountability group will help you thrive in that pursuit.

Sin strongholds retain their power most fully in the darkness of nonadmission. The enemy does not want to you to confront your sin. But if he cannot keep you from confronting your sin, he will encourage you to confront it in private by instilling fear, anxiety, or shame. If he cannot keep you from confessing it to God, he will keep you from confessing to a group. Be aware as these feelings creep in; view them as obstacles to overcome rather than reasons to retreat.

Do Not Let the Sun Go Down on Your Sin

Do not let the sun go down on your anger. (Eph. 4:26)

A healthy practice that my wife and I have in our marriage is to never let the sun go down without clearing up any unresolved hurts between us. We simply refuse to go to sleep if we are mad at each other. Sleep does not solve the hurt; ignoring it does not make it go away. Instead, time turns unforgiveness into bitterness. Left unchecked, bitterness becomes a root that destroys the relationship as it grows deeper and deeper.

> *Strive for peace with everyone, and for the holiness without which no one will see the Lord. See to it that no one fails to obtain the grace of God; that no "root of bitterness" springs up and causes trouble, and by it many become defiled.* (Heb. 12:14–15)

There have been two or three times in our more than thirty years of marriage that we have violated this rule. And we regretted it each time. Not only did the tension remain, but the morning brought deepened hurt—both the pain of the original offense and the pain of not trying to resolve it. Those two or three times have underscored for us the importance of not letting the sun go down on our anger.

You should be *quick* to root out sin in your life in the same way. When you recognize sin, confess it immediately to God. If you have offended someone, be quick to confess it to him or her as well and seek forgiveness. Make it a habit not to let the sun go down on any unconfessed sin. Rob the sin of its power to plant bitterness into your life and your relationships.

Put on the Holy Opposites to Build a Life of Righteousness

Your Father's goal is not simply to root out sin in your life. He wants you to have a holy lifestyle—the fallow ground for the Spirit to fill you and guide you.

Much of this chapter has dealt with the first part of the rooting-out sin process described in Ephesians 4:

1. **Put off** an old sin (sinful habit/practice) (Eph. 4:22)
2. **Renew your mind** (change how you think) (Eph. 4:23)
3. **Put on** the holy opposite (godly habit/practice) (Eph. 4:24)

To build a life of holiness and righteousness, however, you must actively put on the holy opposite of every sin God roots out. To be free of a sin, you cannot simply remove it from your life. Unless it is replaced by something good and holy, it will come back again, usually worse than before.

> *"When the unclean spirit has gone out of a person, it passes through waterless places seeking rest, but finds none. Then it says, 'I will return to my house from which I came.' And when it comes, it finds the house empty, swept, and put in order. Then it goes and brings with it seven other spirits more evil than itself, and they enter and dwell there, and the last state of that person is worse than the first. So also will it be with this evil generation."* (Matt. 12:43–45)

Just as the S.W.A.P. process seeks supernatural interaction and filling by the Holy Spirit, its converse is true. A lack of this process opens our lives up to supernatural *demonic* influences. Removal of sin, sweeping the house of your heart clean, is not holiness. It is just the first step. Demonic forces in your life create more bondage than before when you confess sin yet fail to change your lifestyle to actively develop holy habits in that area.

Look at one example of sin and its holy opposite:

> *"You have heard that it was said, 'You shall love your neighbor and hate your enemy.' But I say to you, Love your enemies and pray for those who persecute you, so that you may be sons of your Father who is in heaven. For he makes his sun rise on the evil and on the good, and sends rain on the just and on the unjust." (Matt. 5:43–45)*

> *"But I say to you who hear, Love your enemies, do good to those who hate you, bless those who curse you, pray for those who abuse you." (Luke 6:27–28)*

You can confess your hatred to God and receive His forgiveness. In that moment of confession, He can break the power of bondage of hatred and enmity. But if you do not replace it with active loving, forgiving, praying for, and blessing your enemies, the hatred will return worse than before.

This part of the process is a vital step on the path to righteousness, but it's a step you must take each time you confess. You must actively replace sin after sin with holy opposites. This is the manner in which you work out your salvation—your righteous lifestyle. Confession alone cannot transform your life.

> *Therefore, my beloved, as you have always obeyed, so now, not only as in my presence but much more in my absence,* ***work out your own salvation with fear and trembling,*** *for it is God who works in you, both to will and to work for his good pleasure.* (Phil. 2:12–13, emphasis added)

Putting on holy opposites, or habits of righteousness, is like strapping on a breastplate to guard yourself from future assaults of the enemy in certain areas of your life. By doing this, you fill the house of your heart with holy habits that actively counter temptations you are trying to overcome.

Sometimes the holy opposites are obvious. In the passage above, the opposite of hating your enemies is loving, doing good for, blessing, and praying for them. If the Bible does not make it clear what the holy opposite of a sin in your life is, then a good place to start is with the fruit of the Spirit.

> *But the fruit of the Spirit is love, joy, peace, patience, kindness, goodness, faithfulness, gentleness, self-control; against such things there is no law. And those who belong to Christ Jesus have crucified the flesh with its passions and desires.* (Gal. 5:22–24)

Frequently scan the fruit of the Spirit and evaluate if one of these, if actively employed in your life, could help you overcome a particular temptation. For example, I have a friend who overcame a life-long stronghold in a counterintuitive way: by giving thanks for it. Since the Bible says to give thanks for all things (Eph. 5:20), he and his wife began to do so. This robbed the sin of its power.

Beginning the Spirit Trek

In the S.W.A.P. process, the "S," "W," and "A" all lead to the "P"—Pursue the promptings. Putting on the holy opposites is the beginning of learning to walk with the Spirit, learning to keep in step with Him. Just as you must learn to keep in step with a wilderness guide, so you must learn to keep in step with the Spirit.

The whole point of the S.W.A.P. process is to develop a life of holiness, filled with and led by the Spirit of the Almighty God. As you work through the **S**urrendering process, **W**aiting in prayer process, and **A**voiding sin process, you are positioning yourself to be filled afresh with the Spirit. This was all preparation for the Spirit Walk. The promptings He will give you may be unexpected but will always bring joy to you and glory to God.

Now you are ready to take the next step. Let the trek begin!

Questions to Ponder

1. Relate any recognition of desensitization in your life, such as things you once felt were sinful but have gradually accepted. According to God's Word, is it still sinful?

2. Review the holiness path one must take (put off the old sin, renew your mind, put on the holy opposite) to get to the place where the Holy Spirit can begin to fill you. Where do you tend to do well and where do you tend to struggle with these three commands?

3. Paul has given eleven examples of sin (though there are many more) in Ephesians 4:17–5:21. Has one of those particularly struck a nerve with you? What needs to be put off? What needs to change in your thinking? What is the holy opposite you need to put on?

4. Is there something you need to confess to a trusted group of same-sex disciples so that you can be free from it?

5. Is there something you need to confess to someone you have offended (or been offended by) to forgive and be forgiven to avoid a root of bitterness?

CHAPTER 8

S.W.A.**P.** – P̲URSUE THE PROMPTINGS OF THE SPIRIT

The first three aspects of the S.W.A.P. framework are three parts of the same process that leads to the final step and goal of the framework: being led by the Spirit in power. The Spirit is inviting you to the daily, hour-by-hour dance of walking in step with Him—the Spirit Walk.

> **S**urrender to His will and His every word
> **W**ait on God in prayer
> **A**void sin and let God root out all unrighteousness
> **Pursue the promptings of the Spirit**

As you work through the process outlined in the previous chapters, whether in a longer period of time away with God (SWAPmeet) or a daily time alone with Him, the process should culminate with an invitation to the Spirit to fill you afresh. Your heavenly Father wants to give His Spirit to you in fullness. He is not reluctant. He is waiting for you to come as a surrendered son or daughter to Him and to ask Him for a fresh filling.

All you have to do is ask.

The Spirit Ask

Giving you the Holy Spirit in fullness (not just to indwell you) is the heart of your Father. When you know your heavenly Father's heart, you can ask Him without doubting and receive from Him what He promises. Most of the promises of Scripture are conditional: you must say "yes" to God in certain ways to receive what He has promised. The previous chapters have been about what your Father asks of you in order to entrust His Spirit to you in fullness. As you surrender yourself to those commands of Scripture, then your heart is ready to receive a fresh filling of His Spirit. [insert image Quote Call Outs_32>]

At this point in the S.W.A.P. process, you are a ready vessel. All you need to do now is to ask your Father to fill you again with His Spirit. He loves to pour out His Spirit on surrendered children.

> And I tell you, **ask, and it will be given to you**; seek, and you will find; knock, and it will be opened to you. **For everyone who asks receives**, and the one who seeks finds, and to the one who knocks it will be opened. What father among you, if his son asks for a fish, will instead of a fish give him a serpent; or if he asks for an egg, will

> *give him a scorpion? If you then, who are evil, know how*
> *to give good gifts to your children, **how much more will***
> ***the heavenly Father give the Holy Spirit to those***
> ***who ask him!*** (Luke 11:9–13, emphasis added)

Here is the promise from your loving Father: "Submit to Me. Then ask Me to fill you. I will come to you and not leave you as an orphan!" Just as you love to give good gifts to your children, so God wants to give the gift of His Spirit to you.

All you have to do is ask.

Jesus promised never to leave you as an orphan, but to send His Spirit.

As you meet the conditions of surrender and confession, God loves to draw near to you. This process of surrender and confession can take days or minutes depending on your starting point. But the process is always the same, and James has clearly outlined that process. Observe the elements of S.W.A.P. in this passage:

> *Or do you think that the Scripture speaks to no pur-*
> *pose: "He jealously desires the Spirit which He has made*
> *to dwell in us"? But He gives a greater grace. Therefore it*
> *says, "GOD IS OPPOSED TO THE PROUD, BUT GIVES GRACE TO*
> *THE HUMBLE." Submit therefore to God [SURRENDER].*
> *Resist the devil and he will flee from you. Draw near to*
> *God and He will draw near to you [WAIT IN PRAYER].*
> *Cleanse your hands, you sinners; and purify your hearts, you*

*double-minded [AVOID SIN]. Be miserable and mourn
and weep; let your laughter be turned into mourning and
your joy to gloom. Humble yourselves in the presence of the
Lord, and He will exalt you [PURSUE PROMPTINGS
as He raises you up].* (James 4:5–10, NASB)

If you have followed the process outlined in the previous chapters (and in James 4:5–10), you should expect God to respond with a fresh filling of His Spirit. Ask Him and He will fill you. Remember, this is no "name it and claim it" theology. The fullness is entirely dependent on your posture of surrender.

Pray to Him from your heart something like this:

THE SPIRIT ASK

"Dear Father in heaven, as your child, I have done my best to surrender myself to You and Your purposes. I have sought Your forgiveness of all my sin and I desire to live a pure life. Today I want to know You better, live for You wholeheartedly, and serve Your purposes. Please fill my entire being now with your Holy Spirit. As Your precious child, I receive your filling by faith. Help me to follow Your promptings. Thank you!"

When you ask your Father to fill you, you should expect Him, in faith, to do so. At times, when the Spirit fills you, you recognize a tremendous difference. Sometimes experiencing Him afresh is dramatic, as is this case of the disciples who had already been filled once in Acts 2:

> *And when they had prayed, the place in which they were gathered together was shaken, and they were all filled with the Holy Spirit and continued to speak the word of God with boldness.* (Acts 4:31)

At other times, His filling presence is like a gentle whispering wind and your soul is filled with peace that He is guiding and speaking to you.

> *And he said, "Go out and stand on the mount before the Lord." And behold, the Lord passed by, and a great and strong wind tore the mountains and broke in pieces the rocks before the Lord, but the Lord was not in the wind. And after the wind an earthquake, but the Lord was not in the earthquake. And after the earthquake a fire, but the Lord was not in the fire. And after the fire **the sound of a low whisper**. And when Elijah heard it, he wrapped his face in his cloak and went out and stood at the entrance of the cave. And behold, there came a voice to him and said....* (1 Kings 19:11–13, emphasis added)

Do not expect God to show up in fullness the same way twice. His presence does not follow some prescription or formula. Rather, He comes to you in the way you need Him at the moment—sometimes quite dramatically and other times with no physical manifestation. Trust God to come to you as He knows will be best.

Similarly, never expect Him to demonstrate His filling the same way twice or for Him to prompt you in the same manner as He did previously. Since He is God, only He knows the steps He will guide you to take.

> *The heart of man plans his way, but the LORD establishes his steps.* (Prov. 16:9)

Some believers will tell you that the sign of being filled with the Spirit is speaking in tongues, prophesying, or some other spectacular gift. They may tell you that it is a one-time occurrence, and that once you're filled, you're always filled.

But this not only goes against the teaching of the Bible but the very nature of the relationship you have with a living God. God does not conform Himself to some formula or set pattern. The Spirit of the living God is going to come to you in various ways and prompt in you various emotions and responses. Sometimes it will feel dramatic, and other times it won't.

Regardless, receive the filling of the Spirit by faith and begin following the promptings of His Spirit as He directs. As I personally ask the Spirit to fill me for the day, I rise from my daily quiet time in faith that He is guiding me. At times, I physically sense that God has worked in me powerfully. More often, I receive His presence by stepping out of the boat, like Peter, in faith (Matt. 14:29).

Often, God will fill you with His Spirit *before* you ask Him. This was the case with many disciples in the Bible as they assumed the S.W.A.P. posture. How many times have we found that in a time of fresh surrender, a time of worship in His presence, or a time of travail, His Spirit falls

~~us~~ on us in power—convicting, comforting, encouraging, teaching, illuminating?

Sometimes you just receive this filling at God's initiative and timing. But never be afraid to ask. This is your heavenly Father's heart. Ask Him like a child does with a daddy.

The Spirit Walk

Remember, the Holy Spirit already dwells in you if you are a believer in Jesus Christ. You do not have to beg God to give you the Spirit. He is in your life and always will be.

But this is different from being *filled* with the Spirit. The goal is to walk in the fullness of the Spirit, led by Him in every way. The goal  is to let Him control your life to enable you to overcome every problem, conquer every sin, find guidance in each decision, receive help in every need, and make an impact around you for the kingdom of God.

Your goal is to walk by the power and guidance of the Spirit moment by moment. This is the Spirit Walk.

The Example of Jesus

The Spirit Walk is how Jesus walked every day. He was led by the Spirit of God in every moment. He is our example to follow:

> *So Jesus said to them, "Truly, truly, I say to you, the Son can do nothing of his own accord, but only what he sees the Father doing. For whatever the Father does, that the Son does likewise. For the Father loves the Son and shows him all that he himself is doing. And greater works than these will he show him, so that you may marvel.* (John 5:19–20)

Jesus followed the promptings of the Father that came through the Spirit of God. The Spirit was the voice of His Father, prompting Him at each step.

> ***The Spirit*** *immediately drove him out into the wilderness.* (Mark 1:12, emphasis added)

> *And Jesus,* ***full of the Holy Spirit****, returned from the Jordan and was led by the Spirit in the wilderness.* (Luke 4:1, emphasis added)

> *And Jesus returned* ***in the power of the Spirit*** *to Galilee, and a report about him went out through all the surrounding country.* (Luke 4:14, emphasis added)

> *[Jesus] unrolled the scroll and found the place where it was written,*

> ***"The Spirit of the Lord is upon me****, because he has anointed me*

to proclaim good news to the poor.
He has sent me to proclaim liberty to the captives
and recovering of sight to the blind,
to set at liberty those who are oppressed,
to proclaim the year of the Lord's favor."
And he rolled up the scroll and gave it back to the at-
tendant and sat down. And the eyes of all in the syna-
gogue were fixed on him. And he began to say to them,
"Today this Scripture has been fulfilled in your hear-
ing." (Luke 4:17–21, emphasis added)

In that same hour ***he rejoiced in the Holy Spirit*** *and said,*
"I thank you, Father, Lord of heaven and earth, that you
have hidden these things from the wise and understand-
ing and revealed them to little children; yes, Father, for such
was your gracious will. (Luke 10:21, emphasis added)

The Message of Acts

Jesus's disciples followed His example in the Book of Acts. In more than fifty occasions in twenty-eight chapters, the Spirit is mentioned as working in and guiding the early Christ-followers (not just the Apostles). Receiving the Spirit on the day of Pentecost was just the beginning of a day-by-day guidance by the Spirit. The Spirit's guidance—the Spirit Walk—was the undeniable mark of God's power in the lives of the early believers.

*Then Peter, **filled with the Holy Spirit**, said
to them....* (Acts 4:8, emphasis added)

*They were all **filled with the Holy Spirit** and
continued to speak the word of God with boldness.* (Acts 4:31, emphasis added)

*Therefore, brothers, pick out from among you seven men of
good repute, **full of the Spirit** and of wisdom, whom we
will appoint to this duty.* (Acts 6:3, emphasis added)

*But they could not withstand the wisdom
and **the Spirit with which [Stephen] was
speaking**.* (Acts 6:10, emphasis added)

*But [Stephen], **full of the Holy Spirit**, gazed into heav-
en and saw the glory of God, and Jesus standing at the
right hand of God.* (Acts 7:55, emphasis added)

*And **the Spirit said** to Philip, "Go over and join
this chariot."* (Acts 8:29, emphasis added)

*And when they came up out of the water, **the Spirit of the
Lord carried Philip away**, and the eunuch saw him no more,
and went on his way rejoicing.* (Acts 8:39, emphasis added)

*And while Peter was pondering the vision, **the Spirit
said** to him....* (Acts 10:19, emphasis added)

*While Peter was still saying these things, **the Holy Spirit fell on all who heard the word**. (Acts 10:44, emphasis added)*

*"And **the Spirit told me** to go with them, making no distinction." (Acts 11:12, emphasis added)*

*And one of them named Agabus stood up and **foretold by the Spirit** that there would be a great famine over all the world (this took place in the days of Claudius). (Acts 11:28, emphasis added)*

*While they were worshiping the Lord and fasting, **the Holy Spirit said**, "Set apart for me Barnabas and Saul for the work to which I have called them." (Acts 13:2, emphasis added)*

*So, being **sent out by the Holy Spirit**, they went down to Seleucia, and from there they sailed to Cyprus. (Acts 13:4, emphasis added)*

*But Saul, who was also called Paul, **filled with the Holy Spirit**, looked intently at him. (Acts 13:9, emphasis added)*

*And the [new] disciples were **filled with joy and with the Holy Spirit**. (Acts 13:52, emphasis added)*

*And when Paul had laid his hands on them, **the Holy Spirit came on them**, and they began speaking in tongues and prophesying. (Acts 19:6, emphasis added)*

> *And now, behold, I am going to Jerusalem, **constrained by the Spirit**, not knowing what will happen to me there, except that the Holy Spirit testifies to me in every city that imprisonment and afflictions await me.* (Acts 20:22–23, emphasis added)

> *Pay careful attention to yourselves and to all the flock, in which **the Holy Spirit has made you overseers**, to care for the church of God, which he obtained with his own blood.* (Acts 20:28, emphasis added)

The emphasis of the Book of Acts is that you cannot live the life God has called you to without the guiding power of the Spirit. Rather, God has called *ordinary* disciples to live on mission, and has provided His Spirit as the means to do that with holy, maturing character. He was the Hidden Mover of Acts. The Acts record provides examples of disciples committed to the Spirit Walk.

The Biblical Equation of the Spirit Walk

S.W.A.P. is the posture we assume to start the Spirit Walk. Acts demonstrates the equation for the ongoing nature of the Spirit Walk:

Living for the MISSION and PURPOSE of God

+

Relying on the POWER and GUIDANCE of the SPIRIT each moment

WALKING IN THE SPIRIT
(victorious Christian living and fruitful ministry)

In a passage that vividly describes the way Paul and his team lived by the kingdom equation, the guidance of the Spirit is evident. Paul and his missionary team were surrendered to the mission the Father had given them but needed guidance and power on when, where, and how.

> And they went through the region of Phrygia and Galatia, having **been forbidden by the Holy Spirit** to speak the word in Asia. And when they had come up to Mysia, they attempted to go into Bithynia, but **the Spirit of Jesus did not allow them**. So, passing by Mysia, they went down to Troas. And a vision appeared to Paul in the night: a man of Macedonia was standing there, urging him and saying, "Come over to Macedonia and help us." And when Paul had seen the vision, immediately we sought to go on into Macedonia, concluding that God had called us to preach the gospel to them. (Acts 16:6–10, emphasis added)

To engage in any serious ministry to spread God's kingdom, you need the unwavering guidance and empowerment of the Spirit. Otherwise, your methods, tools, spiritual disciplines, and projects are lifeless motions.

The key to any effective ministry is combining the guidance and power of the Hidden Mover with solidly biblical ministry tools. The key to a victorious Christian life is not simply breaking free from sin bondages and old baggage and "believing" you can stay free. Rather, it is combining the guidance and power of the Spirit with the biblical disciplines that help you overcome sin, navigate trials, put on holy habits, and be fruitful in ministry.

- *Overcome sin:* Without reliance upon the Spirit, the biblical admonition to "flee youthful lusts" is fueled by your willpower. Willpower alone will never conquer most sins.

- *Navigate trials:* Without reliance upon the Spirit, you will never give thanks *in* and *for* all things, particularly trying circumstances. When difficult news gut-punches you, you will revert to complaining, worrying, and muddling forward in the darkness of your own strength.

- *Put on holy habits:* Without reliance upon the Spirit, putting on the holy habits that result in a changed character will remain elusive. Though you may find yourself occasionally thinking, speaking, and doing the right things, more frequently you will revert to old ways. Words that you regret. Thoughts that wander into wrong arenas. Old habits that won't die.

- *Be fruitful in ministry:* Without reliance upon the Spirit, you will find that even great ministry tools and plans lack power. You miss the people God has set you up to meet. Your methods and meanderings become mere mechanics.

Live for the Mission and Purpose of God

The Acts record emphasizes that ordinary disciples lived by the Spirit Walk equation—living for God's mission by the power of the Spirit. They received the Spirit in fullness *precisely because* they lived for the mission Jesus had given them. For three years, many of these disciples had seen the example of Jesus and heard His admonitions to live for the Father's mission.

> *"The Son of Man came to seek and to save the lost."* (Luke 19:10)

> *Jesus said to them, "My food is to do the will of him who sent me and to accomplish his work. Do you not say, 'There are yet four months, then comes the harvest'? Look, I tell you, lift up your eyes, and see that the fields are white for harvest."* (John 4:34–35)

> *And Jesus said to them, "Follow me, and I will make you become fishers of men." And immediately they left their nets and followed him.* (Mark 1:17–18)

> *When [Jesus] saw the crowds, he had compassion for them, because they were harassed and helpless, like sheep without a shepherd. Then he said to his disciples, "The harvest is plentiful, but the laborers are few; therefore pray earnestly to the Lord of the harvest to send out laborers into his harvest."* (Matt. 9:36–38)

> *And Jesus came and said to them, "All authority in heaven and on earth has been given to me. Go therefore and make*

> *disciples of all nations, baptizing them in the name of the Father and of the Son and of the Holy Spirit, teaching them to observe all that I have commanded you. And behold, I am with you always, to the end of the age."* (Matt. 28:18–20)

> *"And this gospel of the kingdom will be proclaimed throughout the whole world as a testimony to all nations, and then the end will come."* (Matt. 24:14)

> *"But you will receive power when the Holy Spirit has come upon you, and you will be my witnesses in Jerusalem and in all Judea and Samaria, and to the end of the earth."* (Acts 1:8)

Many of us attempt to drive the car of the life God has given us, but we do not point it toward the right destination—His mission and purposes. The Acts disciples received power *for* the mission. When you do not align your life to the mission of God, you do not receive power for the mission. The Spirit Walk equation falls apart:

Living for YOUR OWN purposes
+
Seeking the POWER and GUIDANCE of the SPIRIT
each moment

NO SPIRIT FULLNESS
(disempowered Christian living)

You cannot walk in the Spirit if you do not live for the mission and purposes of God. Why should God fill you with His Spirit if you choose not to live for His purposes? If the mission of what He is doing in history is unclear and your part in it seems murky, you are probably not surrendered to His purposes. If you choose to live for your own desires, your own glory, and your own pleasures, God will not pour out His Spirit in power. His power always accompanies His purposes.

The most powerful and common promptings of the Spirit are related to helping you live for the purposes of God. His promptings are always aligned with His mission.[11]

Rely on the Power and Guidance of the Spirit Each Moment

Unfortunately, even when you get your life on track and begin driving down the highways of His purposes, it is easy to fail to do so with His power. Just as you lived for your own purposes in your own strength, you can attempt to live for God's purposes in your own strength. That equation does not work either. Without the fullness of the Spirit, your gas tank is on empty, even as you attempt to drive toward His mission.

---

11 : For further reading about the idea of the mission and promptings of God and how they relate, see the parable "The Father's Rescue Van" at the end of the book.

Living for the MISSION and PURPOSE of God
+
Relying on YOUR POWER each moment

WALKING IN FRUSTRATION
(no breakthrough; human-sized results)

Like Jesus and the early disciples, you are called to follow the promptings of the Spirit and rely upon His moment-by-moment guidance. When He fills us, the Holy Spirit—as a person—speaks to us just as any other person does. Since He is a spirit and not a physical person, you need to tune your ears to hear His voice and follow His leadership. As you do so, He will help you fulfill the purposes of God with growing, transformed character. Your soul was created with a Spirit-shaped receptacle; you were designed to walk in His power. When He is plugged into your life, your walk overcomes the plans of the enemy.

This is when the Spirit Walk begins to thrill your soul! You are returning to the design of the Creator who walked in the cool of the day with Adam (Gen. 2:15; 3:8). You are following in the footsteps of godly predecessors like Moses who pointed the way to a more intimate walk with God.

Thus the LORD used to speak to Moses face to face,
as a man speaks to his friend. (Ex. 33:11)

When Moses came down from Mount Sinai, with the two
tablets of the testimony in his hand as he came down from the
mountain, Moses did not know that the skin of his face shone
because he had been talking with God. Aaron and all the people
of Israel saw Moses, and behold, the skin of his face shone,
and they were afraid to come near him. (Ex. 34:29–30)

Communing with God through the daily guiding of the Hidden Mover is what you were designed for. Walking in the Spirit returns you to the Creator's plan. The Spirit Walk sets you on the path to steward the mission the Redeemer has given you.

The attitudes and actions described in this book lead to an exhilarating lifestyle, which goes by various names:

- Walking in the Spirit
- Abiding in Christ
- Being led by the Spirit
- Letting the word of Christ richly dwell within you

Only then can you fulfill the high design of the Christian walk:

I appeal to you therefore, brothers, by the mercies of God, to
present your bodies as a living sacrifice, holy and acceptable
to God, which is your spiritual worship. Do not be conformed
to this world, but be transformed by the renewal of your
mind, that by testing you may discern what is the will of God,
what is good and acceptable and perfect. (Rom. 12:1–2)

Only by the Spirit Walk can you live with all of the power of God working mightily within you.

> *Him [Christ] we proclaim, warning everyone and teaching everyone with all wisdom, that we may present everyone mature in Christ. For this I toil, struggling* **with all his energy that he powerfully works within me***. (Col. 1:28–29, emphasis added)

> *For I will not venture to speak of anything except what Christ has accomplished through me to bring the Gentiles to obedience— by word and deed, by the power of signs and wonders,* **by the power of the Spirit of God***—so that from Jerusalem and all the way around to Illyricum I have fulfilled the ministry of the gospel of Christ.* (Rom. 15:18–19, emphasis added)

The key to overcoming every problem in your life and growing in Christlikeness is the fullness of the Spirit.

The key to power in ministry and lasting fruitfulness is the fullness of the Spirit.

The key to transformed, healthy relationships is the fullness of the Spirit.

You began your life by the power of the Spirit. In exactly the same manner, you must grow as a follower of Jesus and fisher of men through the power of the Spirit filling and guiding you.

> *Oh, foolish Galatians! Who has cast an evil spell on you? For the meaning of Jesus Christ's death was made as clear to you as*

> *if you had seen a picture of his death on the cross. Let me ask you this one question: Did you receive the Holy Spirit by obeying the law of Moses? Of course not! You received the Spirit because you believed the message you heard about Christ. How foolish can you be? After starting your new lives in the Spirit, why are you now trying to become perfect by your own human effort? Have you experienced so much for nothing? Surely it was not in vain, was it?* (Gal. 3:1–4, NLT)

It does not make sense to start by the Spirit then cower from following the promptings of the Spirit in your Christian life. You must live the rest of your days the same way you began: by the power of the Spirit. To do so, you must follow His promptings as He fills you.

How does He prompt you?

When He Fills You, He Speaks to You

When the Holy Spirit fills you, He begins to speak to you. Since the Spirit is a spirit, not a physical person, you most likely will not hear an audible voice. Rather, you will sense the Spirit of Jesus prompting and speaking to you in different ways. Remember, God has already spoken clearly in His inspired Word, the Bible. Most often, the Holy Spirit will speak to you through emphasizing various parts of the Bible at various times. It is difficult to hear the Holy Spirit speak when you do not spend time daily reading the Word of God. It is hard to hear the Holy Spirit speak when you do not know the Word of God in your heart. Knowing the

Word of God is the foundation for hearing the voice of the Spirit. This is why it is vital to maintain the life-giving practices of daily quiet time and periodic SWAPmeets.

Helping you know and remember Jesus's words is a core role of the Spirit. He is your Teacher to help you live out the Word:

> *But the Helper, the Holy Spirit, whom the Father will send in my name, he will teach you all things and bring to your remembrance all that I have said to you.* (John 14:26)

> *But the anointing that you received from him abides in you, and you have no need that anyone should teach you. But as his anointing teaches you about everything, and is true, and is no lie—just as it has taught you, abide in him.* (1 John 2:27)

In addition to bringing Scripture to your mind, the Holy Spirit will speak to and prompt you in other ways. But these promptings will *always* be consistent with the Bible. They will never run counter to what God's Word says. Evaluating a prompting by whether it conforms to God's Word is a good test of whether that prompting is from the Holy Spirit, from your own imagination, or from some other source.

- Perhaps He will bring an image to mind that you must respond to.

- Perhaps He will put a mission or errand on your heart for that day.
- Perhaps He will put a specific message on your heart to be shared with someone.
- Perhaps He will convict you of a change you need to make.
- Perhaps He will put a song of praise on your heart that bubbles out of your lips.
- Perhaps He will reveal something to you about someone that you should share with that person.
- Perhaps He will put a need in someone's life that you should meet through your actions.
- Perhaps He will put an idea in your mind that you cannot shake.
- Perhaps He will put a phrase in your mind that repeats until it makes sense.

However He does it, the Father will reveal to you His purposes and plans. All He asks you to do is join Him in the part He gives you, just as Jesus did.

So Jesus said to them, "Truly, truly, I say to you, the Son can do nothing of his own accord, but only what he sees the Father doing. For whatever the Father does, that the Son does likewise. For the Father loves the Son and shows him all that he himself is doing. And greater works than these will he show him, so that you may marvel." (John 5:19–20)

> *"If you love me, you will keep my commandments. And I will ask the Father, and he will give you another Helper, to be with you forever, even the Spirit of truth, whom the world cannot receive, because it neither sees him nor knows him. You know him, for he dwells with you and will be in you. I will not leave you as orphans; I will come to you…. In that day you will know that I am in my Father, and you in me, and I in you. Whoever has my commandments and keeps them, he it is who loves me. And he who loves me will be loved by my Father, and I will love him and manifest myself to him…. If anyone loves me, he will keep my word, and my Father will love him, and we will come to him and make our home with him."* (John 14:15–18, 20–21, 23)

As you obey Jesus's commands out of love, your life becomes a well-swept home worthy of the presence of God. God begins to show you what He is doing. You will have clearer spiritual eyes to see His work and finer-tuned spiritual ears to hear His promptings.

The Bible calls these promptings that result in Spirit-empowered actions "the manifestation of the Spirit." The word "manifestation" in the Greek just means "disclosure, revelation, revealing, unveiling, appearing." In other words, the Spirit will begin to unveil ways for you to live by His power so that you can serve God and others.

> *To each is given the **manifestation** of the Spirit for the common good. For to one is given through the Spirit the utterance of wisdom, and to another the utterance of knowledge according*

to the same Spirit, to another faith by the same Spirit, to another gifts of healing by the one Spirit, to another the working of miracles, to another prophecy, to another the ability to distinguish between spirits, to another various kinds of tongues, to another the interpretation of tongues. All these are empowered by one and the same Spirit, who apportions to each one individually as he wills. (1 Cor. 12:7–11, emphasis added)

Notice how each action here is prompted by the Spirit. These are just some of the examples of how the Spirit might lead you. The Spirit prompts you and you begin to act.

The Fear Factor

Precisely at this point, fear attacks many believers. Their gut instinct is to label such phenomena as charismatic or Pentecostal. They fear that saying "yes" to the Spirit will make strange things happen, or that following the promptings will immediately slap a religious label on them that they don't want. Some recoil because following the promptings of the Spirit simply takes them out of their comfort zone.

Suppose you have just taken the arduous routine of S.W.A.P.: Surrendering, Waiting in prayer, Avoiding sin and asking the Spirit to fill you. Your path to fullness has been through saying, "Yes, Lord."

How tragic if your first response to the Prompting of the Spirit is, "No!"

HOW TRAGIC IF YOUR FIRST RESPONSE TO THE PROMPTING OF THE SPIRIT IS, "NO!"

Saying "no" grieves the Spirit of the Master and you must start the S.W.A.P. process over again. **Promptings are the avenue of walking with God.** He speaks. You say "yes."

Just as Jesus could only do the things His Father showed Him, your goal should be to do everything the Father shows you. He manifests and you move in response. Regardless of what anyone would think or say about Him, Jesus followed every prompting of His Father. Since the Holy Spirit truly is the Spirit of Jesus (Acts 16:7), you become like Jesus!

Remember, promptings are not confined to actions that society has labeled as "strange" or "sensational." Promptings can include a sudden urge to say hello to someone on the sidewalk, a sense that you should ask your server at a restaurant if you can pray for him or her, a conviction to stop to help a broken-down motorist, or even unrelenting whispers that a friend needs you, immediately. Banish fears; the promptings move you to become more Christlike.

Promptings for His Glory

The things God will reveal to you always bring Him glory. The Spirit's role is to bring glory to Jesus. The ways He prompts you to act will also bring the greatest glory to Jesus.

> *"When the Spirit of truth comes, he will **guide you** into all the truth, for he will not speak on his own authority, but*

*whatever he hears he will speak, and **he will declare to you** the things that are to come. **He will glorify me**, for he will take what is mine and **declare it to you**. All that the Father has is mine; therefore I said that **he will take what is mine and declare it to you**.* (John 16:13–15, emphasis added)

The things the Spirit declares are for the purpose of enabling you to bring glory to God and serve His purposes. God wants you to live for his agenda.

Remember, too often we ask the wrong question: "What is God's will for my life?" The center of this question is us, not God.

The right question is simply, "What is God's will?" Period.

Then we must ask, "How can my life best fit into that and bring God the greatest glory?"

The Father is delighted to show you His purposes and prompt your steps when you are surrendered. Every prompting He gives you will fit in with that purpose. The Father does not prompt you by His Spirit simply for the fun of it. He prompts you in order that you may live for His glory. He will keep clarifying his mission and purpose for you at each stage of your life as you live for His fame.

Promptings for Your Good as Well

The amazing thing is that God's promptings are not only for His glory but also for your greatest good. As your Creator, God knows how to perfectly weave together His glory and your good in the path He outlines for you. Since He created you, He knows what is best for you.

> *For you formed my inward parts;*
> *you knitted me together in my mother's womb.*
> *I praise you, for I am fearfully and wonderfully made.*
> *Wonderful are your works;*
> *my soul knows it very well.*
> *My frame was not hidden from you,*
> *when I was being made in secret,*
> *intricately woven in the depths of the earth.*
> *Your eyes saw my unformed substance;*
> *in your book were written, every one of them,*
> *the days that were formed for me,*
> *when as yet there was none of them.* (Ps. 139:13–16)

When God saved you through His grace, your salvation did not catch Him by surprise. Since before the foundation of the world, He ordered your steps. Matching your steps to His plans brings you the greatest joy in life.

> *For by grace you have been saved through faith. And this is not your own doing; it is the gift of God, not a result of works, so that no one may boast. For we are his workmanship, created in Christ Jesus for good works,* ***which God prepared beforehand, that we should walk in them.*** (Eph. 2:8–10, emphasis added)

Therefore, my beloved, as you have always obeyed, so now, not only as in my presence but much more in my absence, work out your own salvation with fear and trembling, for it is God who works in you, both to will and to work for his good pleasure. (Phil. 2:12–13)

Since walking in step with the Spirit is like an earthly marriage, let me share with you an example that may take away the fear of saying "yes" to His promptings.

A few years ago, when we lived in Singapore, my wife and I returned from a multi-week trip. After pouring ourselves out in training God's workers and investing in the lives of people in multiple countries, we came home exhausted. With an especially heavy speaking and teaching load, I was unusually spent.

As previously mentioned, our tradition each morning is to wake up early and drink coffee in bed together. On our first morning waking up in our own bed, Laura said, "Honey, let's do something that will be refreshing *especially for you*. What would you like to do?"

Immediately I thought about Singapore's amazing cinemas and Western restaurants. After weeks of local cuisine, I was ready for something different. I thought, "It would be awesome to go see a guy flick on a monster screen and eat a juicy burger!"

Instead of throwing that out there, I asked her, "I don't know, honey. What would you suggest?"

She said, "Why don't we go to the Botanic Gardens and walk around?"

Hmm. Not what I had in mind. Not even close!

Don't get me wrong. Singapore is a beautiful tropical island state. Because it's near the equator, flowers bloom there constantly. But when she mentioned this, I began to envision us walking among the flowers, lying on our backs in the grass, and watching the clouds go by. Not nearly as exhilarating as an action movie!

I now had two options to this prompting from my wife:

Option one: "You want me to do what?! Are you crazy?!"

Option two: Anything else revolving around the word "yes."

Option one would have spoiled the moment and provided a distinct tenseness in our relationship.

Somehow, God gave me the grace to choose option two. Out of my lips came the words, "Sure, honey, that sounds great!"

Do not be deceived by that exclamation mark. Frankly, I was not excited by this prompting by my wife. I knew better what I wanted for that day—our first day off in a long time.

After coffee and breakfast, we made our way to the Botanic Gardens. Sure enough, my expectations—fears!—were certainly fulfilled. What did we do?

We wandered among the flowers.

We lay on our backs,
   held hands,
      watched the clouds go by,
        and just talked.
           And, to my surprise, it was perfect.

Lying there in the grass, watching the clouds, my spirit revived. Life-giving sap surged through my mind and body. The flowers spoke to a place of hunger. The lingering with my beloved answered a call to intimacy. The glory of God's creation filled a hole unfillable by human devices.

In that moment, as life spread through my being, I realized that someone knew me better than I knew myself. The promptings of my beloved could be trusted. My beloved had my welfare at heart.

A guy flick and a juicy hamburger were life-stealing counterfeits for the true refreshment I needed that day. How much better to follow the promptings of my beloved in times like this.

I realized she knew what was best for my life. Her promptings gave me life! An action movie and a juicy hamburger would not have refreshed me. I thought I knew what was best for me. But someone else there knew me better. How much better to follow her promptings on days like this.

And we did get some delicious nachos and fajitas afterward at a lively restaurant. As I said, my beloved knows me.

Your Creator knows you inside and out. He knows every cell in your body. He knows every thought. In creating you for His glory, He also promises to act for your good, to conform you to the design you were made for—the image of Christ.

> *And we know that God causes all things to work together for good to those who love God, to those who are called according to His purpose. For those whom He foreknew, He also predestined **to become conformed to the image of His Son**, so that He would be the firstborn among many brethren.* (Rom. 8:28–29, NASB, emphasis added)

When you love God and live for His purposes, He works every circumstance for your good. He is a compassionate Father. When His Spirit prompts you, it is always going to bring you the greatest joy. It will always be life-giving.

Like me with my wife following our trip, you have two options in your response to His promptings:

Option one: "You want me to do what?! Are you crazy?!"

Option two: Anything else revolving around the word "yes."

Even if what the Spirit tells you sounds counterintuitive to your thinking, say yes. God knows what you need more than you do. He knows how He made you. Following His promptings is the most life-giving exercise of your life. Option two gives life.

Option one robs you of life and joy.

> *The sorrows of those who have **bartered for another god** will be multiplied…. You will make known to me the path of life;*
> *In Your presence is fullness of joy;*
> *In Your right hand there are pleasures forever.*
> (Ps. 16:4, 11, NASB, emphasis added)

Psalm 16 explains why God's people are so often filled with sorrow and powerlessness. They have bartered God's ways for another god in their life. Any time I find myself lacking joy, I ask myself the question: "Have I prioritized another god in my life?" These gods can be power, achievements, hobbies, ventures, relationships, materialism, sex, escapism, ambition, esteem, wrong views of God—anything that you put more joy and confidence in than God.

Have you bartered for anything other than the God of the Bible?

The call of this book is to *reverse barter*. Trade the wrong thing for the right thing, like I traded an action movie and a burger for life-giving time with my wife. Swap your control for His. When you do, you will find fullness of joy in His presence.

You do not need to fear God's promptings. His promptings are the best thing for you. His promptings are the best thing for the people around you. C. S. Lewis explained it quite graphically: "We are half-hearted creatures, fooling about with drink and sex and ambition when infinite joy is offered us, like an ignorant child who wants to go on making mud pies in a slum because he cannot imagine what is meant by the offer of a holiday at the sea. We are far too easily pleased."[12]

To Stay Full of the Spirit, Keep Saying "Yes"

The goal in being filled with the Spirit is a nonstop Spirit Walk. The hope is to go as long as you can in the fullness of the Spirit without grieving Him. You want to stay in close, listening, trusting mode as long as possible.

Your goal should be to say "yes" to each successive prompting. Say "yes" and "yes" and "yes" again. Never say "no" to the Spirit. The longer you say keep saying "yes," the longer you walk in the Spirit. Rather than walking in the Spirit for minutes, you want to abide in Him for hours and days.

To abide for long periods of time, you must S.W.A.P. throughout the day. S.W.A.P. is not an exercise restricted to multi-day retreats and daily quiet times. It is a *lifestyle*. It should be like breathing. To be led by the Spirit, keep reminding yourself to stay surrendered. Each choice gives you the chance to let Him be Master or for you to become master again.

> S.W.A.P. IS NOT AN EXERCISE RESTRICTED TO MULTI-DAY RETREATS AND DAILY QUIET TIMES. **IT IS A LIFESTYLE. IT SHOULD BE LIKE BREATHING.**

---

12 C. S. Lewis, *The Weight of Glory* (San Francisco: HarperOne, 2001), 26.

Wait on Him in prayer as you make choices—even if just for a few seconds. When people ask a friend of mine to pray for them, my friend takes a few seconds first to pray about how to pray. That is being led by the Spirit.

A big part of this is living on-mission to avoid any hint of sin throughout the day. Each temptation should be met with a choice to flee sin and put on the holy opposite. As you remain a clean vessel, the Spirit of holiness is delighted.

Throughout the day ask the Spirit to fill you and prompt you, whether in making a business decision or a ministry visit. Until you are able to use decisions themselves as the trigger to check in with the Spirit, set reminders on your phone (perhaps a simple alarm that goes off each hour), on sticky notes on the fridge and bathroom mirror, or reminders wherever you'll see them. Pause, ask the Spirit to prompt you, and say "yes" immediately.

S.W.A.P. must be the *posture* of your life.

> *And do not get drunk with wine, for that is debauchery, but be filled with the Spirit.* (Eph. 5:18)

If you do use your phone as a reminder, you can give it a special ringtone that will prompt you to stay surrendered to the Spirit's control. Do this for a season and you may set some new patterns of abiding in Christ.

Inevitably, you will say "no" to the Spirit at some point. When you do—offending Him by choosing your own way—you have grieved the Spirit and must be filled again. How far you have wandered from God's holy way will determine how long it will take you to work through the S.W.A.P. process again—to make up with your Master.

Walking in the Spirit is like developing a muscle in your body. At first, it may be difficult and you may fail often. Over time, however, you should be able to train your spirit to surrender to the Spirit, and to *stay* surrendered for longer stretches. Each time you fail, simply S.W.A.P. to receive fresh filling.

The Most Common Promptings

What do you think was the most common visible sign or prompting by the Spirit as believers in the New Testament were filled afresh with the Spirit? The answer may surprise you.

It was *not* speaking in tongues, though that is a common perception. The Bible makes it clear that not all Spirit-led believers will speak in tongues. That is just one gift among many others.

> *All are not apostles, are they? All are not prophets, are they?*
> *All are not teachers, are they? All are not workers of miracles,*
> *are they? All do not have gifts of healings, do they?* **All do**
> **not speak with tongues, do they?** *All do not interpret,*
> *do they?* (1 Cor. 12:29–30, NASB, emphasis added)

So what was the one common sign that believers were filled with the Spirit in the Book of Acts? Was there a prompting they *all* received?

Speaking the Word of God with Boldness

The answer is yes. The inevitable sign that accompanied every filling of the Spirit was that the believers **spoke the word of God with boldness** in some manner.

> *And when they had prayed, the place in which they were gathered together was shaken, and they were all filled with the Holy Spirit and **continued to speak the word of God with boldness**.* (Acts 4:31, emphasis added)

If you are looking for one common sign of the Spirit of Jesus filling you, it is likely that you want to speak about Jesus boldly and confidently—praising Him, telling others about Him, giving testimony of His power in your life, and so on. When my wife and I take one of our mini-honeymoons, we draw close in a fresh way. When we get back to normal life, the fires of intimacy remain. I cannot help but talk about her to myself, to her, and with anyone I meet. The more enamored, in love, and appreciative of her I become, the more I want to talk about her.

When we fall freshly in love with Jesus, and He fills us with His presence, we want to talk about him to anyone we meet. This is a sure sign of whether the Spirit is filling you or not. Do you speak openly about Him with both believers and nonbelievers?

Ephesians 5 lists results that come from being filled with the Spirit. Speaking about the Lord was actually the very first prompting listed and is mentioned several ways:

> *And do not get drunk with wine, for that is debauchery, but be filled with the Spirit, **addressing** one another in **psalms** and **hymns** and spiritual **songs**, **singing** and making melody to the Lord with your heart, **giving thanks always** and for everything to God the Father in the name of our Lord Jesus Christ, submitting to one another out of reverence for Christ. (Eph. 5:18–21, emphasis added)*

When the Spirit fills you, you want to sing about your Lord, speak about your Lord, and give thanks to Him always. You speak the Word of God with boldness. This is different from speaking in a language that no one understands. This is talking clearly about your Beloved to Him (praising and worshiping Him), to yourself (reminding yourself how amazing He is, filled with gratitude about your salvation), and to others (sharing with them testimonies, verses from the Bible, a simple gospel presentation, and so on.)

Giving Thanks FOR All Things

Another frequent sign (or prompting) of being filled with the Spirit is also mentioned in Ephesians 5:20, and it is just a subset of speaking about God boldly:

> **Giving thanks** always and **for everything** to
> God the Father in the name of our Lord Jesus
> Christ. (Eph. 5:20, emphasis added)

Many believers know they are supposed to give thanks *in* all things:

> Give thanks **in all circumstances**; for this is the will of God
> in Christ Jesus for you. (1 Thess. 5:18, emphasis added)

Giving thanks in all circumstance is an important discipline. That you can still praise God and give him thanks no matter the circumstance is a huge act of faith in the goodness of God (Rom. 8:28–29).

But the Bible tells you not only to give thanks *in* everything, but *for* everything. Giving thanks for everything is an even greater act of faith. Thanking God for everything, even the difficult and tragic things, demonstrates in a deeper way that you trust in His goodness and sovereignty as a heavenly Father. No human being can live this way consistently unless prompted to do so by the Holy

Spirit. Only the Holy Spirit can lead you to live a life of thankfulness in and for every circumstance.

It's important to note that gratitude is largely absent in the downward spiral of sinful societies. In the Romans 1 progression of the depravity of man, the slippery slope of sin and perversion begins with not praising God or giving Him thanks.

> *For although they knew God, they **did not honor him** as God or **give thanks** to him, but they became futile in their thinking, and their foolish hearts were darkened.* (Rom. 1:21, emphasis added)

Failing to honor God and give Him thanks is an indicator that you think you know better. When you do that, you are elevating your thinking over His wisdom. Do this repeatedly and it becomes a lifestyle that spirals further away from God.

Thanking and praising God for every circumstance of your life is critical for walking in the Spirit. It is an act of faith to help you walk in the Spirit.

Love and Mutual Submission

The final manifestation or sign of being filled with the Spirit in Ephesians 5 is that you seek the welfare of others by living in mutually submissive relationships, otherwise known as "love." You love others and submit to them because you revere Christ. He is in control of you.

*Submitting to one another out of
reverence for Christ.* (Eph. 5:21)

Too many followers of Jesus assume that manifestations of spectacular gifts of the Spirit are the only signs of being filled with the Spirit. You will, over time, learn to exercise the gifts He gives you. But the goal of every gift is that it may build up the body.

*So with yourselves, since you are eager for manifestations of the
Spirit, strive to excel in building up the church.* (1 Cor. 14:12)

The gifts of the Spirit are poured out upon the church. You have special ones that God has given you. But the gifts are not the only promptings God will give you. Obedience to any prompting of the Spirit—even those that feel unspectacular—brings great glory to God.

Some of the most mundane acts may be the most Spirit-prompted because they are reminders by God to live out the commands of His Word. God prompting you to walk upstairs and comfort a child is just as clearly a prompt from Him as a miraculous healing. God prompting you to care for a homeless person on the corner is just as certainly a prompting as doing some spectacular work for God. God prompting you to walk across the street to share the good news with your neighbor is just as surely a move of His Spirit as a word of prophecy.

Love is the sure sign of being full of the Spirit. It is the first fruit of the Spirit mentioned in Galatians 5:22. Serving

others, submitting to them, loving them above yourself—
these are indicators that God is in control. Sandwiched
between the two remarkable chapters on the gifts of the
Spirit (1 Corinthians 12 and 14) is the "more excellent
way"—1 Corinthians 13.

> *And I will show you a still more excellent way*. *If I speak
> in the tongues of men and of angels, but have not love, I
> am a noisy gong or a clanging cymbal. And if I have pro-
> phetic powers, and understand all mysteries and all knowl-
> edge, and if I have all faith, so as to remove mountains, but
> have not love, I am nothing. If I give away all I have, and
> if I deliver up my body to be burned, but have not love, I
> gain nothing.* (1 Cor. 12:31–13:3, emphasis added)

The promptings of the Spirit, whether sensational or mundane, will always be guided by love. You will know that you
are on the path to following the promptings of the Spirit if
each act demonstrates love toward God and love toward
the people around you, including those who seem unlov-
able. When you want to serve their needs over your own
and submit to their desires more than your own desires,
you are probably walking in the Spirit. You have the love
of the Father abiding in you.

> *No one has ever seen God; if we love one another, God
> abides in us and his love is perfected in us. By this we know
> that we abide in him and he in us, because **he has given***

*us of his Spirit…. So we have come to know and to be-lieve the love that God has for us. **God is love, and who-ever abides in love abides in God, and God abides in him**. (1 John 4:12–13, 16, emphasis added)*

The Most Common Results: Fruit of the Spirit

The signs just mentioned are some of the immediate signs of being filled with the Spirit. This list is not exhaustive. As you learn to walk in the Spirit over time, the most common results are not gifts that you exercise in the body, as important as they are. Learning to use the gifts the Holy Spirit gives you is critical in the Christian life. Many books have been written about this subject.

But the most common result of a continuous, steady walk in the Spirit is that you bear the fruit of the Spirit. You live with a transformed character.

But the fruit of the Spirit is love, joy, peace, patience, kind-ness, goodness, faithfulness, gentleness, self-control; against such things there is no law. And those who belong to Christ Jesus have crucified the flesh with its passions and desires. (Gal. 5:22–24)

Love, joy, peace, patience, kindness, goodness, faithful-ness, gentleness, and self-control do not sound nearly as exciting as prophecy, miracles, and healings. Yet they are the sure mark the Spirit is filling you. They are the fruit of the Spirit Walk.

Prolonged obedience to the Spirit's promptings produces the maturity of life that God has designed for you. Walking in the Spirit produces Christlikeness.

Many of us seek the fruit of the Spirit without seeking the *source* of the fruit—the Spirit. If you want to be **loving**, do not strive to be loving. Instead aspire to be filled with the Spirit.

If you long for **patience**, do not work harder to be patient. Rather, be filled with the Spirit.

If you want more consistent **self-control** in your life, do not seek after self-control. Rather, let the Spirit fill you.

The Spirit is the source of the fruit. Surrender to the control of the Spirit and the fruit will result.

Read again the email I received from a fellow missionary after listening to and applying messages on S.W.A.P. At this point in the book, his words make even more sense.

It was the concise nature in the way you presented the information.

I've heard, done, and experienced all of the elements before and have had short times of being filled but it never lasted long. It was always elusive and mysterious. So many pastors just throw it out there—"be filled with the Spirit"—but give no real guidance on how to do it. Not that it is a 3-step process but there are critical components.

Now that I have experienced being filled for a longer period of time, I truly understand that the fruit of the Spirit (Love, Joy, Peace...) becomes effortless to execute since He is doing it and it is not from my flesh. I've spent many years trying to have the fruit of the Spirit through the power of my own effort. To be sure, I asked God for help to exhibit the fruit but I was not S.W.A.P.ing, not giving it all. Working for the result (the fruit) but not the cause (being filled).

Effortless to execute. How could it be said better?

Do you long for the fruit of the Spirit in your life? If so, walk in the Spirit day by day, hour by hour. As you walk in the Spirit, the fruit will grow more mature in your life:

deeper **love**
    fuller **joy**
        abiding **peace**
            longsuffering **patience**
                selfless **kindness**
                    unstained **goodness**
                        dependable **faithfulness**
                            power-filled **gentleness**
                                sin-conquering **self-control**.

The Invitation

Do you long for the fruit of the Spirit in your life?
Do you long for growing, godly character?
Do you long for victory over sin?

Do you long for fruit in your ministry?
Do you desire to make some great impact for God?
Do you hunger to know God more intimately?
Do you aspire to bring Him fame?

The biblical path to each of these is the Spirit Walk. The steps toward the path are simple enough to jot down on a napkin in your favorite coffee shop: S.W.A.P. Whether in extended times with your Master or while driving to your next errand, just keep S.W.A.P.ing. Make the simple steps to a lifestyle that leads to an unpredictable path. He is the Hidden Mover behind all you do.

Surrender to His will and His every word
Wait on God in prayer
Avoid sin and let God root out all unrighteousness
Pursue the promptings of the Spirit

Jesus stands before you, arms stretched out wide, calling to you, His beloved, in a loud voice:

"If anyone thirsts, let him come to me and drink. Whoever believes in me, as the Scripture has said, 'Out of his heart will flow rivers of living water.'" Now this he said about the Spirit, whom those who believed in him were to receive, for as yet the Spirit had not been given, because Jesus was not yet glorified. (John 7:37–39)

Will you heed the call to the Spirit Walk? Your Savior wants to flow through you like rivers of living water. You were designed for this.

Abiding in Christ
Being filled with the Spirit
Letting the word of Christ richly dwell within you
Being led by the Spirit

Each describes the same path: **the Spirit Walk**, the ancient, forgotten way.

It was the familiar way of the Acts generation. It is the well-trodden trail of disciples in movements all over the globe.

From the beginning to the end of the Bible, this was the path you were designed for:

BEGINNING: The Spirit Walk was God's design at creation in Genesis 1.

MIDDLE: The Spirit Walk is the call throughout Scripture.

END: The Spirit Walk is the final call of the last chapter of the Bible.

The Spirit and the Bride say, "Come." And let the one who hears say, "Come." And let the one who is thirsty come; let the one who desires take the water of life without price. (Rev. 22:17)

**Accept the invitation.
Come and drink!**

Questions to Ponder

1. Have you been surprised by the answer to the greatest sign of the Spirit-led life—being prompted to speak the Word of God boldly and with love? Examine your life. How have you experienced boldness in telling others about Jesus? Do you praise Him often? Do you relate to others in a loving way?

2. What other promptings of the Spirit described in this chapter were a surprise to you? What felt refreshing when you read it?

3. How have you been surprised by joy in saying "yes" to a prompting you wanted to say "no" to? Share with others your experience.

4. Contemplate (and share with others) a time when you obeyed a prompting by God that manifested His Spirit in a way that completely exceeded your expectations.

5. Review "The Father's Rescue Van" at the end of the book. Where are you in that story? Where would you like to be in that story?

CONCLUSION

The Spirit Walk is essential—not optional—for every believer who wants to live out and serve God's perfect design. The Spirit Walk must become our standard operating procedure. Walking in the Spirit should be the most *natural* aspect of our *supernatural* life.

But we must never assume that the S.W.A.P. process of the Bible—the ancient path that has been forgotten—is understood by believers, including us. Spirit Walk amnesia abounds. No follower of Jesus naturally stumbles into the Spirit Walk. It takes conscious, faith-filled effort.

In the minds of most Christians, missionaries head the top of their lists of the godliest people on earth. Surely, of all Jesus followers, *they* must naturally walk in the Spirit.

Having worked as a missionary and with missionaries for twenty years, I have learned not to assume that even they understand the Spirit Walk.

Return to the Hidden Mover

For several years, my wife and I led five hundred missionaries in Southeast Asia. God was rocking our world about how to return to ancient biblical methods in practical ways to go into the dark places of our region to lead people to Jesus, help them grow as disciples, form them into healthy churches, and equip many to become leaders. We explored and implemented ways to help these new believers and churches repeat the process so they could become disciple-makers as well. The goal was that this pattern would continue generation after generation with new disciples—just like in the book of Acts.

Breakthroughs emerged in many parts of our region. Our godly personnel were encouraged. One soon-to-retire missionary came to me with tears in his eyes and said, "I wish I had known these things forty years ago." Choking back the tears, he continued, "But I am resolved to live this way when I return to America."

Our ministry went well for a while, but soon most of our teams sputtered at about the first or second generation of new churches. Disciples were not consistently multiplying and churches were not getting to the third or fourth generation.

By and large, our five hundred missionaries were stuck. The root of the problem was that Plan A—the Spirit Walk— was not clear. We were implementing the *principles* of Acts but not in the *power* (and Person) of Acts.

I had *assumed* that these dear colleagues understood the Spirit Walk which must take precedence over the Self

Walk. But most of them had never been taught how to walk in the Spirit. *For breakthrough to occur in ministry, breakthrough had to start with us. We had forgotten the Hidden Mover behind the methods!*

For the next two years, that set me on a path to travel from team to team, meeting to meeting, to share the S.W.A.P. process. Many expressed that it was the *first time* they had really understood practically how to walk in the Spirit. Conviction came to many missionaries and national pastors that they were living more in the power of the Self Walk than the Spirit Walk. Repentance resulted in humble efforts to start S.W.A.P.ing daily, to exercise the muscle of surrendering to the Spirit's control.

In the months that followed, our personal breakthroughs resulted in ministry breakthroughs. First- and second-generation disciples and churches began to birth children, grandchildren, and great-grandchildren churches. Soon, third- and fourth-generation churches were not uncommon. One brother wrote me recently that they are now tracking eighteen generations of new churches in one Muslim people group!

Acts is happening again! The *extraordinary* power— the *extraordinary* Person—of Acts is available for *ordinary* people.

The Hidden Mover wants to bring breakthrough in your personal life so that you return to God's perfect design and truly become like Christ. The Father wants to empower your transformed life to make a difference in this broken world. The only route to both of these—a transformed life and the power to make a difference—is the Spirit Walk. The path is simple to understand, but takes conscious effort to walk out.

Take the Courageous Journey with Hungry Friends

But walk it you can, especially with a group of spiritually hungry believers around you to work through this process together.

One of the reasons brides have bridesmaids and grooms have groomsmen is to keep their faith strong leading up to the wedding hour! In the back rooms of the chapels and churches as brides nervously put

> ONE OF THE REASONS BRIDES HAVE BRIDESMAIDS AND GROOMS HAVE GROOMSMEN IS TO **KEEP THEIR FAITH STRONG LEADING UP TO THE WEDDING HOUR!**

on make-up and grooms nervously straighten their ties once more, close friends speak reassuring words.

"She is the right one. Don't forget that."

"You made a great choice. This journey will be awesome."

In such a supportive environment, as the hour strikes, the wedding party assembles to walk the aisle with confidence and joy.

You need such friends to help you walk the aisle of the sweetest relationship you ever dreamed of—your marriage to God.

Courageously walking the aisle and starting the journey with your friends may be the beginning of a revival not only in your life, but in your church and community. The fires of revivals throughout history have been sparked by such small groups.

One of the greatest mission movements in history started this very way. In 1806 five students at Williams College in Massachusetts began praying together regularly during a time of revival in America. One afternoon, these five men discussed and prayed about William Carey's booklet *An Inquiry into the Obligation of Christians to Use Means for the Conversion of the Heathen*. It was a call to ordinary believers to surrender to the call to take the gospel to the unreached places of the world by the extraordinary power of the Spirit. Their hearts were especially gripped by the thought of China's lost millions.

In the midst of their discussion a deafening thunderstorm rushed upon them, catching them unawares. Quickly the five students fled to the shelter of a haystack. Beneath the cover of the haystack, an argument arose because of the danger of such an enterprise. Samuel Mills called the group to prayer. With loud peals of thunder overhead, he prayed that God would strike down any objection to His will.

With the storm still raging, Mills then looked at his fellow students and cried out, "We can do this, if we will!" Spiritually something broke in that moment. The five all pointed back to this event as the watershed moment in their lives. Binding themselves together encouraged each to attempt something for God he might not otherwise. Extraordinary power in ordinary people.

The sacrifice and example of this small band launched the first North American mission organization and eventually inspired 100,000 college students to surrender to God's mission in the Student Volunteer Movement.

When the people of God gather to seek God unreservedly and unhindered, God shows up in power.

And when they had prayed, the place in which they were gathered together was shaken, and they were all filled with the Holy Spirit and continued to speak the word of God with boldness. (Acts 4:31)

Our Christian society is rife with examples of shallow discipleship and untransformed Christian lives. It is time for us to return to life-changing discipleship rooted in the Spirit Walk. Let's S.W.A.P. our control for God's.

Surrendering to His will and word.
Waiting on Him in prayer.
Avoiding sin and letting Him root out all unrighteousness.
Pursuing the promptings that He then gives.

The Spirit of Jesus awaits you, ready to fill you daily, so that you can return to the forgotten paths. It's a call for you to empty yourself of your own control and let the Spirit of Jesus take over.

> And [Jesus] said to all, "If anyone would come af-
> ter me, let him deny himself and take up his
> cross daily and follow me." (Luke 9:23)

With a hungry band of travelers, trod the self-denying trail of the Spirit Walk.

The Spirit stands ready to empower you. He is not reluctant. He eagerly desires to lead you in this journey. All you must do is surrender, ask, and drink:

> *"If anyone thirsts, let him come to me and drink. Whoever
> believes in me, as the Scripture has said, 'Out of his
> heart will flow rivers of living water.'" Now this he said
> about the Spirit, whom those who believed in him were
> to receive, for as yet the Spirit had not been given, be-
> cause Jesus was not yet glorified.* (John 7:37–39)

It was the call Jesus gave during his earthly ministry and it is the same call to the final generations. From first to last, all of Scripture calls you to the ancient paths:

> *The Spirit and the Bride say, "Come." And let the one who hears
> say, "Come." And let the one who is thirsty come; let the one
> who desires take the water of life without price.* (Rev. 22:17)

Come.
Drink.
Walk.

FORMAT FOR A SWAPMEET: MULTI-DAY, DAILY, HOURLY

Distilling the ideas from this book, three simple guides are presented here to serve as a skeletal structure for SWAPmeets. This is your opportunity to take time with your Father to go through the S.W.A.P. process. Remember, the purpose is to help you S.W.A.P. your control for His so that the Spirit fills you afresh and then guides you down the path.

These guides are not a science or a prescription. Your aim is an encounter with God to more deeply root yourself in Him. Since God does the filling, we cannot dictate the timing. But He is delighted to fill His children with His Spirit when they humble themselves before Him.

Use these guides as a foundation for three SWAPmeet time frames, where you'll meet God to exchange your control for His. Remember, these guides are not the law—they are just guidelines. Feel free to make any adjustments that help you follow biblical patterns.

Multi-Day SWAPmeet

Choose a time frame that is the *maximum* you can, not the minimum you can. This time frame allows you to work through bigger life issues than you can normally get through in your daily quiet time. Be sure to schedule a multi-day SWAPmeet when you see your love growing cold, when you know you need a deeper work of God, or when you need direction for the next stage of life.

Remember, a married couple can often tell when they need time away with each other. The sparks settle, even dull, and it's clear a new honeymoon is needed. Similarly, your spiritual fires will dim from time to time. Let flickering light be a sign they need to be stoked—that it is time to get away again.

HOW LONG: 2–7 Days

Most people can manage more than one day away with God. One and a half to two days would be the minimum I'd recommend. You may even want to go beyond seven days if God directs you to. The key is listening to Him and doing all you can to clear the time and space for Him to do what He desires.

WHERE: A Place Where You Will Not Be Disturbed

Find a cabin in the woods, a house at the beach, a secluded hotel, the house of a friend who is traveling—anywhere you will not easily be disturbed. Consider also doing a total technology fast during your time with God—no internet, no texting, no social media, no email. Giving people electronic access to you can be as distracting as staying at a place where people can easily find you. I recommend turning on the "do not disturb" function on your phone and only allow one or two close family members or friends to get through to you in case of emergency.

Send out a text and email notification to friends, family members, and colleagues (and turn on a vacation responder) to let them know you will be unavailable during this time.

You may want to consider doing a physical fast for all or part of your time.

WHO: Either by Yourself, with a Spouse/Friend, or with a Few Friends Who Hunger to Meet God

If you know you are prone to wander in your time with God, invite someone (or a group of Spirit-minded friends) who can help you stay on track in meeting with God each hour and each day. If friends are more of a distraction or would hinder you from opening up completely to God, then go by yourself. You'll just want to make sure you have a way to hold yourself accountable.

SUPPLIES: Bible (Physical), Journal, Pen, Markers/Colored Pencils for Your Bible, and Some Way to Search the Bible (Online Concordance, Phone App, Printed Concordance)

Journaling is a key part of the S.W.A.P. process. You could use a computer, tablet, or phone, but if you do, turn off their Internet capability to avoid distraction.

Many find great pleasure in going "old school"—using a real, printed Bible and a paper notebook. You may want to buy a special Bible just for your SWAPmeets so you've got all of your important takeaways in one place. Do not be afraid to highlight your Bible and write in the margins. Let God speak to you.

HOW: Set Your S.W.A.P. Pace According to the Exact Amount of Time You Have

Pre-SWAPmeet Detox

If you are going for more than two days, and you have been exhausted from work/life, you may want to begin your time with some rest and recreation. I find that if I am burned out or exhausted, I sometimes need a day or two just to "detox" from the demands of life. During this time you will need to sleep, eat well, get some exercise out-doors (go for a walk by a body of water if possible), wor-ship the Lord, and pray. Just relish having time away with God. At some SWAPmeets, I have had to start by staring at a lake, a forest, or the ocean for hours on end, loving my Lord and relaxing in Him. Until I did that, I was not ready to move to the harder work of diving into the S.W.A.P. pro-cess. Just remember, a detox time is *not* a time to sim-ply distract yourself with other gods (Psalm 16:4). This is a time to relax in the Lord and draw your heart to Him. **Read**

Psalm 16 in multiple translations throughout this time, meditating on the Lord as your inheritance.

S.W.A.P. Process

Rhythm
Build a rhythm for going through the S.W.A.P. process following your detox. Do not press yourself to rise too early and stay up too late if your mind and body are tired. If the Lord is speaking to you late into the night, stay up with Him. If you need to sleep in the next morning, do so. If God wakes you up early in the morning to speak to you, get up and listen. But do not be afraid to go to bed early that night if you need to. Let your loving Father guide the pace of your time with Him.

Purpose
Throughout the process keep focusing on these aims:

"Father, I just want to know You better and love You more. Please reveal Yourself to me. Show me Your glory!" (see Ex. 33:18)

"Father, I want to know what You are doing in my generation and bring great glory to You with my life. Show me Your will and how

I can serve that. Make Yourself famous through me." (see John 12:28)

"Father, I long for you to show me any way that my life does not conform to You and help me to be transformed into Christlikeness." (see Ps. 139:23–24; Rom. 12:1–2)

◆ ◆ ◆

Write these purposes on pieces of paper and keep them in your Bible, in your journal, and in a prominent spot you will see, like on your bathroom mirror. Let them serve as the themes to which you continually return.

Expectancy

Realize that, as a Father, God wishes to give you His Spirit fully (see John 3:34). He is not reluctant. Here are a few more verses to print or write out and read through periodically on your retreat.

> *And I tell you, ask, and it will be given to you; seek, and you will find; knock, and it will be opened to you. For everyone who asks receives, and the one who seeks finds, and to the one who knocks it will be opened. What father among you, if his son asks for a fish, will instead of a fish give him a serpent; or if he asks for an egg, will give him a scorpion? If you then, who are evil, know how to give good gifts to*

your children, how much more will the heavenly Father give
the Holy Spirit to those who ask him!" (Luke 11:9–13)

He gives the Spirit without measure. (John 3:34)

Expect that God will fill you with His Spirit at the right time. *Ask* Him to fill you throughout your time. Review the parable of the Persistent Widow (Luke 18:1–8), which starts this way:

And he told them a parable to the effect that they ought always
*to pray and **not lose heart**.* (Luke 18:1, emphasis added)

Process

When you have several days away, the easiest way to work through the S.W.A.P. process is to pick a place in the Bible to read (a book of the Bible or a theme in the Bible) and to go through S.W.A.P. as you read. Use the Bible as your starting point.

Consider these options when choosing a book of the Bible to read through:

- A Gospel – Looking at the life of Jesus and His teaching is always a great place to start.
- Romans – Many major revivals and reformations have begun by reading the book of Romans.
- Epistles – You might choose an epistle that speaks to your situation (1 John – love; Philippians – joy;

Ephesians – a mini-Romans; James – practical kingdom advice).

- Acts – Let God rock your view of what He can do.
- Old Testament book – You might want to add to your New Testament reading an Old Testament book such as Exodus, Nehemiah, Joshua, Psalms, or one of the prophetic books (like Isaiah) which call the people back to God.

This is a **BASIC PATTERN** that might be helpful:

1. **Read a large chunk of Scripture (several chapters):** Make notes in your Bible and especially in your journal on what God is teaching you.
2. **Pray and work through S.W.A.P. as you do:** Consciously pray through what you read.
   a. **Surrender:** How do you need to surrender to God's WILL and to every WORD you read? Are you as surrendered as possible at this point?
   b. **Wait in prayer:** Pray back the reality of the Scripture you read and evaluate its impact on your life.
   c. **Avoid sin:** What sins is God pointing out in your life through this process?
      i. Confess them to Him and make steps to get right with others or make restitution as needed.
      ii. Make plans to put on the holy opposite and get help from other friends for sins

you know will require good accountability for true transformation.

    d. **Pursue the promptings:** Ask the Spirit to fill you and to point you to steps you need to take for the next season. Write down any promptings He gives you and make plans to obey these promptings. Say "yes!"

3. **Write down insights, decisions and prayers in your journal:** As you work through a section of scripture, make sure you record what God is telling you.

4. **Follow "rabbit trails" of scripture:** The Holy Spirit, your Teacher, may prompt you to follow "rabbit trails," or cross-references, to other part of the Bible that speak to themes He is bringing to light. Follow these themes. Use a concordance to find those cross-references. *The Treasury of Scripture Knowledge* is a great one-book resource if you do not know the cross-references to pursue.

5. **Repeat the process with the next few chapters of the Bible book you are reading.**

6. **Interlude—Accountability Questions List:** To really root out sin, take the time to work through the accountability questions of the Wesleyan movement found at the end of this book. Many times your Bible reading is enough to do this, but feel free to supplement the Bible with these questions that prompt you to think.

7. **Interlude—Prayers God Delights In:** Use the prayers in Appendix 4 to pray through at various intervals through the days you have.

8. **During each break, review the three main purposes you have printed/written out and put within sight.**

9. **When you are overloaded, get out, enjoy nature, and praise God:** If you find that you are getting overwhelmed or that your brain is feeling overworked, take time to go for a walk. Sing songs of praise to God and enjoy His presence. Your SWAPmeet is not a legalistic time. Let the Spirit prompt you in each exercise of your SWAPmeet. Do not be afraid to rest (or even nap) during your SWAPmeet.

10. **You're done when He is done!** God will give you special peace at some point in this multi-day time with Him. You will sense that you are as surrendered as possible, have confessed all your sins, and are ready to move forward. You will sense that He is filling and guiding your mind and heart. When He signals that you are done, you are done. Thank Him for the filling of His Spirit and walk in joy and freedom to the next steps He has for you. If you finish your SWAPmeet early, fine. Your goal was to meet Him and you did.

A Reminder about Group Interactions

If you are going through the SWAP process with friends, agree to come back together at periodic junctures throughout the day. You can set up a schedule such as every two hours, or at meal times and before bed.

Share highlights from your journal, decisions you have made, sins God has pointed to, and so on. Take time to pray together and to commit to helping each other walk forward in the transformation God is bringing to your lives.

You may want to schedule some time in the morning and evening to worship and praise the Lord together in song.

Together you may want to pray through the prayers that God delights from Appendix 4 and work through the Wesleyan accountability questions in Appendix 3.

Daily SWAP

The goal of your quiet time is to stay full of the Spirit (see Luke 5:16) or, if you have been resisting Him, to surrender to His control. A great way to do this is to turn your daily quiet time into a mini SWAPmeet. As George Mueller did each day, your goal is to "make your soul happy in the Lord."

When you take your time alone with Jesus each day, consciously work through the S.W.A.P. acronym during your Bible reading, journaling, and praying in the same way you'd work through it during a longer time away with God.

If you do not have a normal quiet time pattern, use one like this for fifteen, thirty, or sixty minutes of unhurried time with God:

- READ
  - Choose a **Psalm** (psalms helps you praise and thank God even in difficult circumstances).
  - Read one passage in a book of the **New Testament**, with the goal of reading through this book continuously over several days/weeks until you are done. Do not attempt to read too much. Just read enough to meditate on.
  - If you have thirty or more minutes, considering adding the chapter of **Proverbs** that corresponds to the day of the month (for example,

Proverbs 1 on the first day of the month). Proverbs gives practical wisdom for living.
- JOURNAL: Write down insights God gives you.
- PRAY back the Scripture you have read and the things God has put on your heart.
  - Quickly run through the S.W.A.P. acronym and relate it to the Scripture you have read. Ask the Spirit to fill you and guide you.
  - Pray through a normal prayer list (for family, friends, work, church, mission, the lost, etc.).
- RISE in faith that the Spirit is filling and leading you. Make it your aim to continue to abide in Christ throughout the day, conscious of His presence and following His lead.

Hourly SWAP

To remind yourself to S.W.A.P. throughout the day, as mentioned, you might set your phone alarm to ring every hour, perhaps on the *eighteenth* minute of each waking hour to remind you of Ephesians 5:*18*:

And do not get drunk with wine, for that is debauchery, but be filled with the Spirit. (Eph. 5:18)

You can give it a special alert sound that will prompt you to stay surrendered to the Spirit's control. Do this for a season and you may set some new patterns of abiding in Christ.

When it goes off, quickly ask these questions in your heart:

- *SURRENDER:*
  - *Am I consciously surrendered to Jesus right now?*
  - *Am I full of the Spirit now?*
- *WAIT: Am I awaiting His guidance?*
- *AVOID: Is there any sin I need to confess?*
- *PROMPTINGS: Is there a prompting I should follow?*

FORMAT FOR A CORPORATE SURRENDER MEETING

In churches, organizations, mission teams (short or long term), or even Christian businesses, corporate SWAPmeets can be extraordinarily beneficial. When individuals draw closer to the Spirit and become filled with Him, the group itself fulfills God's purposes on earth. The format for a corporate SWAPmeet may sound similar to revival meetings of the past. And that is not a bad thing. Though this formula could sound stale, it's actually quite the opposite. Many of the old-time revival meetings truly called God's people to a time of repentance and surrender. View this format as a riff on an approach that is tried and true.

Time Frame: Two Days Minimum
A corporate surrender meeting works best when the people of God are able to gather together for at least two full days. The best way to accomplish this might be to hold a weekend retreat, for a Saturday and Sunday at the

church (canceling morning services), or during a holiday weekend.

Though a block of time is ideal, the corporate surrender can be accomplished over a series of several evenings, if that is all the time you can afford. The problem with this, however, is that it'll take more effort. You'll need to account for the distractions of normal life and will need to work hard to establish continuity from the previous encounter with God.

Goal: Encounter God and Respond to Him

Remember that the goal of the time is for God's people to encounter Him in fullness and respond to Him.

Preparation

Most importantly, start a period of fervent prayer and fasting for awakening from God—usually weeks or months ahead of time. Let God speak to you and fill you as you begin to prepare.

If you are working with a planning group, everyone would benefit by reading the little-known book *The Awakening* by Marie Monsen (Kingsley Press, 1959), which is the account of ten years of such meetings stirring missionaries and leaders into a massive awakening that spread across all of China in the early twentieth century. Let that book and this one serve as meeting planning guides. Let

The Awakening prompt you to encourage people to prepare their hearts prior to the SWAPmeet.

Once you know who will be attending, call meeting attendees (as individuals or small groups) to fast one day or even one meal each week in preparation for the meeting—just make sure you also supply resources on how to fast safely.

Encourage those who will attend to read through this book, as individuals or small groups, to completely surrender their hearts to God. Encourage small groups to begin working through the accountability list found in Appendix 3.

Format: Worship, Word, Response, Flexibility

Prescribing a format for a corporate SWAPmeet is difficult because the goal is to allow God's people to encounter Him and respond well. I would suggest dividing the two days as follows:

5–6 sessions: 2.5–3 hours each. For example:
- Day 1
  - Session 1 (morning)
  - Session 2 (afternoon)
  - Session 3 (evening)
- Day 2
  - Session 4 (morning)
  - Session 5 (afternoon)
  - Depart, or Session 6 (evening)

Each session: Worship (20–30 minutes), Word (45–60 minutes), Response (30–60 minutes), Flexibility (30–60 minutes)

Prior to or at the beginning of the last session: Small groups read the interlude section ("The Story Line of History") and discuss how to glorify God in His purposes

Worship

Simple, moving, heartfelt praises to God that focus on the majesty of God should pave the way to listen to the Word of God. But be careful not to make a worship band with a powerful song lineup the focus of your meetings. Simple, authentic worship should be the aim, encouraging focus on the glory of God and surrender to His majesty.

Word

> *Christ loved the church and gave himself up for her, that he might sanctify her, having cleansed her by the **washing of water with the word**, so that he might present the church to himself in splendor, without spot or wrinkle or any such thing, that she might be holy and without blemish.* (Eph. 5:25–27, emphasis added)

Your goal is to let the Word of God (not fancy sermons) wash over the souls of God's people. Most revival starts through large amounts of God's Word bringing conviction and direction to believers.

Let the Word of God speak to the people. Go through large sections of the Word and let it wash over listeners. Have someone (or several people) teach and proclaim the word of God verse by verse for forty-five to sixty minutes at a time. Rather than an eloquent homily, you want someone to simply explain the text of the Bible (so that it convicts) and call people to respond to it. Let the sword of the Spirit do the work of convicting, not the eloquence of men:

> *For the word of God is living and active, sharper than any two-edged sword, piercing to the division of soul and of spirit, of joints and of marrow, and discerning the thoughts and intentions of the heart.* (Heb. 4:12)

> *For Christ did not send me to baptize but to preach the gospel, and not with words of eloquent wisdom, lest the cross of Christ be emptied of its power.* (1 Cor. 1:17)

Free outlines of messages and resources are provided at our website (SteveSmithBooks.com) as a template if you need a place to start.

Response

After each section of teaching the Word, call individuals and small groups to respond to the themes of that section of the Bible.

They may want to spend extended times in **prayer** at the altar or in small groups around these themes, so leave ample time.

Encourage **confession** of sin privately to God. If confession needs to happen before the small group or the whole assembly, allow it to happen. This is where the leader needs to make sure that the group does not move into excessive flaunting of sin but that confession and restoration happen in a healthy and biblical manner.[13]

Call believers to **surrender to God's purposes** that He may be pointing to in the Bible or themes that are rising. For instance, the assembly may decide to join in God's historical story line (see the interlude) in a concrete manner—engaging an unreached people group, reaching out to immigrants in your community, and so on.

The last main session of the two-day meeting should focus on the question, "Where do we go from here?" Allow disciples to form small groups with the goal of ongoing holiness, surrender, and pursuit of God's purposes. Before (or at the beginning of) the last session, have the small groups re-read the interlude section in this book, "The Story Line of History," between chapters 5 and 6,

---

13 You might encourage those who want to confess to the group to come to the elders or leaders first so that they can help discern if and how it would be appropriate to share publicly.

and discuss how they can most greatly glorify God in His purposes.

During each meeting, do not be afraid to call attendees to respond to God in clear ways of confession, surrender, and dedication to the promptings that He gives them.

Flexibility

Flexibility alone—waiting on God to guide—is as much a part of the success of a corporate surrender meeting as anything else. Flexibility is not about leaving time to talk about last night's game. It's about leaving room to follow the Spirit's promptings in the meeting. You will need a leader or group of leaders who know how to follow God's promptings and move the group to each appropriate next step *while* keeping the group from moving into unbiblical conversation or non-Spirit-led responses.

The goal of flexibility is to allow the Spirit to take the group wherever He directs. For instance, if a time of a public confession and revival begins, do not cut it off but be flexible enough to stay for several hours during that time. Whoever is leading the next "section" of the meeting needs to be ready to cancel that section or to postpone it. Remember, it is not vital to get through each section but it *is* vital for the group to encounter God and respond to Him. Just like the Spirit interrupted Peter's sermon at the house of Cornelius, we need to be ready for Him to cut off our portion as He takes over in power.

> *While Peter was still saying these things*, the Holy
> *Spirit fell on all who heard the word. And the believers
> from among the circumcised who had come with Peter were
> amazed, because the gift of the Holy Spirit was poured out
> even on the Gentiles.* (Acts 10:44–45, emphasis added)

Intercession Team

During the hours of the meeting, form a group of intercessors who will pray during the entirety of the two days. You may need to get intercessors to take different shifts. On-site praying is best, but if that will rob those intercessors from being in the meetings, consider asking believers from other churches or organizations to take up this role while you offer to do the same for them when they hold their own SWAPmeet.

ACCOUNTABILITY QUESTIONS FROM THE WESLEYAN MOVEMENT

1. Am I consciously or unconsciously creating the impression that I am better than I really am? In other words, am I a hypocrite?
2. Am I honest in all my acts and words, or do I exaggerate?
3. Do I confidentially pass on to others what has been said to me in confidence?
4. Can I be trusted?
5. Am I a slave to dress, friends, work, or habits?
6. Am I self-conscious, self-pitying, or self-justifying?
7. Did the Bible live in me today?
8. Do I give the Bible time to speak to me every day?
9. Am I enjoying prayer?
10. When did I last speak to someone else of my faith?
11. Do I pray about the money I spend?
12. Do I get to bed on time and get up on time?
13. Do I disobey God in anything?

14. Do I insist upon doing something about which my conscience is uneasy?
15. Am I defeated in any part of my life?
16. Am I jealous, impure, critical, irritable, touchy, or distrustful?
17. How do I spend my spare time?
18. Am I proud?
19. Do I thank God that I am not as other people, especially as the Pharisees who despised the publican?
20. Is there anyone whom I fear, dislike, disown, criticize, hold resentment toward, or disregard? If so, what am I doing about it?
21. Do I grumble or complain constantly?
22. Is Christ real to me?
23. ADDED: Have I been truthful about my answers?

PRAYERS GOD DELIGHTS IN–SAMPLE PRAYERS

The following are prayers extracted from Chapter 5 that may help you seek God's presence. These prayers can serve as a prompt for how to pray in each of these areas.

❖ ❖ ❖

PRAYER TO GLORIFY GOD

Father in heaven, you alone are the King. You alone deserve all the fame on this earth. I deserve none of it. I confess that my ambitions have too often been centered upon myself, my happiness, my control, my reputation, and my name. In my old nature, this was my natural way of living.

But I want to change all of that. It is hard because I don't know what You will say. But I know You are good and loving. Therefore, whatever You speak will be for Your great glory and my great delight. I only want to serve You and make You famous.

So, Father, I am asking You to show me how to make Your name more famous through my life. Glorify Your name through me! Forgive me for asking you, "What is Your will for my life?"

Instead, **show me Your will**. Period. Show me what You are doing in this world in our generation. Let my understanding be based on Your Word and not my own ideas. As You unfold Your will, then would you allow me the privilege of serving You and Your cause in this world? Show me how my life can best serve You and make You most famous.

As Samuel prayed as child, so I pray, "Speak, for your servant hears" (1 Sam. 3:9). I surrender my dreams, aspirations, and hopes to live only for You. Make me someone who makes You famous!

◆ ◆ ◆

PRAYER OF CONFESSION

O Father in heaven, You are righteous and I am not. Like a sheep, I have gone astray from You. My thoughts are not Your thoughts. My own will has taken over in many areas of my life. And that is sin. I confess to You that I am sinful and need Your cleansing power in my life.

Shine Your light on my heart and show me every area in which I have gone astray from You. As David prayed, I pray as well:

Search me, O God, and know my heart!
Try me and know my thoughts!
And see if there be any grievous way in me,
and lead me in the way everlasting! (Ps. 139:23–24)

As You do, I will confess each sin to You and seek Your forgiveness. I want to be a clean vessel to honor You—a vessel in which Your Spirit can live and work.

Clean me thoroughly and make me whiter than snow. Let there be no impure thoughts, no unresolved relationship, and no offense that I have not made right.

I open my life before You right now. Cleanse me from all unrighteousness. Make me right before You.

◆ ◆ ◆

PRAYER OF HUNGER

O Lord, You alone are my portion! You are the only inheritance I want. Wow! How delightful are the boundary lines of my inheritance in You! I delight in You and the portion You have given me in life.

O Father, show me Your glory. Show me more of You. For, I want You, not just Your promises. I want Your presence, not just your presents. I want Your Spirit, not just the fruit of Your Spirit.

◆ ◆ ◆

You are my treasure and my reward. Let me not leave this place without Your clear and majestic presence in my life. I want to know You, the power of Jesus's resurrection, and the fellowship of His sufferings better (Phil. 3:10). Jesus, do not leave me like an orphan, but come to me. I long for Your presence.

Let me delight more in You, and my relationship with You, than in any earthly thing—any achievement, any relationship, any treasure, any aspiration, any interest, any hobby.

Like the man who found the treasure hidden in a field, I sell everything joyfully to have You (Matt. 13:44–45). Oh, give me Yourself! I am hungry. Let me taste and see that You are good! (Ps. 34:8).

◆ ◆ ◆

PRAYER OF SURRENDER

O Father, I have prayed to know Your will. I have asked how my life can bring the greatest glory to You. I have prayed the prayer of glorifying Your name. Now I understand better the implications of what that means. I have counted the cost. I know it will not be easy.

Father, I am scared to surrender. I lack the courage to obey. It is so much easier to do my will rather than Yours.

Yet, with my Lord Jesus, I pray, "Not my will, but Yours!" With clarity, remind me what Your will is and how I can best serve that. As You reveal that to me, give me the courage to say "yes" to You. I want to rise from this encounter with resolve to want Your will more than life itself.

I surrender my fears to You. I surrender my uncertainty. I know You will answer every question in due time. I know You will walk with me down this path, and that gives me great courage. I know that serving You will bring the greatest delight. With Jesus, I say, "My food is to do Your will and to accomplish Your work" (John 4:34).

◆ ◆ ◆

Minister to me with Your angels. Minister to me with Your presence. This decision is not easy. Reassure my heart that surrender is good. Reassure my heart that You will uphold me.

Not my will, but Yours!

◆ ◆ ◆

The Father's Rescue Van

In an effort to save the lives of rural citizens, a doctor moved to a small town and built a hospital. The hospital staff regularly saved the lives of people who were sick or injured. Soon, however, it became apparent that the doctor could not get some people to the hospital fast enough to save them.

To better facilitate the mission of saving lives, the doctor bought his son an old but functioning van. He asked his son to park the van at the hospital. When someone called in with an emergency, his son should drive the van to the person and pick him up to get him back to the hospital for the doctor to treat him. His son was so excited that he could help his father in this way.

To serve the mission, the father even installed a gasoline pump at the hospital so his son would always have enough gas to run the van to remote areas to rescue people. He filled up the van with gas and gave his son the keys. He posted a guard at the gas pump to dispense gas only for rescue missions.

The first day, the son asked his father, "Dad, in order for this van to be most effective, it is going to need a major tune-up at the mechanic shop. May I have enough gas and money to get it fixed?"

The father replied, "Son, I have already filled up the van with gas. If you feel you need to get it tuned up, you'll have to use the gas I gave you." So on the first day, while the father dealt with emergencies and sick people, the son worked on the rescue van.

The next day, the son asked the father, "Dad, in order for this van to be most effective, it is going to need to look like one of those big-city ambulances with a siren, flashing lights, and rescue equipment. In addition, I think it needs to be painted red. Can I have enough gas to go to the city to get it fixed up?"

The father replied, "Son, I have already given you gas to rescue people. But if you feel you need those other things, you'll have to use the gas you have. But please hurry back. Each day there are people to rescue." So on the second day, while the father dealt with emergencies and sick people, the son worked on the rescue van.

The next day, the son asked the father, "Dad, you know that if I am going to rescue people in my van, I am going to need paramedic training and a paramedic uniform. May I have enough gas to go to the city to get my training?"

The father replied, "Son, it is more important that you just start getting people back here to me at the hospital rather than trying to save them by your own efforts. If you feel you need training, you'll just have to use the gas I've already given you to go to the city." So on the third day, while the father dealt with emergencies and sick people, the son worked on his training and bought his new uniform.

The following day, the son said to the father, "Dad, you know that cell phone coverage out here is not good. If I am going to rescue people quickly, it would be good for me to have a satellite phone. That way you could just call me wherever I am and tell me who to save. May I have enough gas to go to the city to get a new phone?"

The father replied, "Son, all you have to do is stay with me at the hospital. When I hear who needs to be rescued, I'll tell you where to go, give you the gas, and let you bring them back here. But if you think you need a fancy new phone, you'll have to use the gas you have to go get it." So on the fourth day, while the father dealt with emergencies and sick people, the son went to buy a new phone.

On the fifth day, the light-adorned, tuned-up, candy-apple-red rescue van parked next to the little hospital ran out of gas. All the townspeople admired the beautiful van and the smiling, well-dressed, well-trained son standing next to it. Gawkers came from miles around to marvel at this new vehicle.

During the following week, everybody wanted the son's help. The son asked his father for enough gas for the van to give Mrs. Jones a ride to the hairdresser, but he said no. The son asked the father for enough gas to help his friend Frank move a load of trash to the town dump, but he said no. The son asked the father for enough gas to take some fifth-grade boys on a fishing trip, but he said no. The son asked the father for enough gas to commute to night college to complete his college degree, but he said no. Finally, the son asked the father for enough gas to drive around looking for a new house that would match his new status, but still the father said no. And all that week, while the father dealt with emergencies and sick people, the son asked for more gas.

The son grew frustrated that he never had enough gas to fulfill his purposes. In anger he went to his father and complained, "Dad, you gave me this van and I have been extremely careful with it. I have repaired it, I have improved it, and I have used it to get myself important training. I have tried to use it to help people and even meet a few of my needs. Everyone agrees that I have the finest quality van in this town. Every day I ask you for enough gas to get done that day what I need to get done, but you never say 'yes.' I need some power to make this van go. As it is, I just feel powerless!"

With great patience the father responded, "Son, we came to this community with one mission:

to rescue people. From the very beginning I have asked you to only do one thing: follow my wishes by taking the van where I tell you, picking up hurting people, and bringing them to me to heal them.

"I have promised you unlimited gas to accomplish that task, and that alone.

"You have been very excited about that task, but have felt that you needed other things to complete that task. All along, I have known that while those things might be good, they are not critical. And every day I deal with life-and-death cases and some people even die before they get to the hospital, because the rescue van is not being used the way it was intended.

"You have become so excited about the rescue van that you have forgotten the mission.

"Son, how many people have you rescued with the van?"

After a long minute of silence, the son replied, "None."

The father looked at the son, tears in his own eyes, and said, "When you are ready to go where I tell you, I will give you all the gas you need to get you there and back. You will be amazed at how well the van will run. But if you refuse to use the van for saving people, you'll have to find your own gas somewhere else."

In the weeks that followed, while the father dealt with emergencies and sick people each day, the son searched the town for others sources of gas for his shiny rescue van, bitter that his father would give him none.

And week by week, while the son went his own way, the father looked for others who would be willing to drive a van to rescue people in need.